MORE ESSAYS IN
LEGAL PHILOSOPHY

# MORE ESSAYS IN LEGAL PHILOSOPHY

## General Assessments of Legal Philosophies

Selected and edited by
ROBERT S. SUMMERS

*Professor of Law*
*Cornell University School of Law*

UNIVERSITY OF CALIFORNIA PRESS

Berkeley and Los Angeles 1971

UNIVERSITY OF CALIFORNIA PRESS
Berkeley and Los Angeles, California

© in this collection
BASIL BLACKWELL, OXFORD, 1971
ISBN 0520-01971-7
Library of Congress Catalog Card Number: 77-149939

Printed in Great Britain

# Contents

# Editor's Preface

The editor wishes to thank both the authors and the publishers who granted the necessary permissions without which volumes of this kind could not appear at all. The author also appreciates the advice and encouragement that the authors gave him in the course of preparing this collection. But it must be stressed that the views expressed by the editor in the introduction are entirely his own, and it is not to be inferred that any contributor to this volume agrees with them in all respects.

This collection of previously published essays is more or less all of a piece: each essay offers a 'general assessment' of much of the relevant work of a major legal philosopher. Essays of this nature are surprisingly rare in the history of this subject. Indeed, it was not possible to include 'general assessments', of the essay variety, on John Austin, Oliver Wendell Holmes, Jr., and John Dickinson. Critiques of the desired genre simply do not exist, though each of these figures is of undeniably great importance in the history of the subject. If this volume arouses any interest in further work of this kind, it will serve a useful purpose.

It is fortunate that the essays which were available and suitable for inclusion assess the work of important philosophers holding widely divergent views. Thus, Bentham (not Austin) was the progenitor of modern 'analytical' studies in legal philosophy. Pound fathered 'sociological jurisprudence'. And Fuller offers a distinctive and provocative kind of 'technological natural law'. A cross-section of vewpoints of this nature enhances the suitability of the collection for use in law school and philosophy department courses and seminars. One obviously sound approach (pedagogically) would be for students first to read the relevant books and articles by, say, Bentham, or Pound, or Fuller, and then the relevant essay, or essays, in this volume.

But in various ways the essays stand alone, too. For example, most of the essays are distinctly critical in tone, and all are written by thinkers interested in modern analytic philosophy. Accordingly, each reflects the critical standards and critical points of view of that philosophical tradition. Indeed, the essays as a whole may be profitably studied for what they reveal in this regard alone; the editor's introduction was prepared with precisely this possibility in mind.

All footnotes have been left in. They may induce readers, particularly beginners, to pursue certain leads with profit.

Finally, the editor wishes to thank Mrs. Barbara A. Haueisen for alert and efficient assistance in preparing the manuscript.

R. S. S.

108 Brandywine
Ithaca, N.Y.

# Notes on Criticism in Legal Philosophy

## ROBERT S. SUMMERS

### I. INTRODUCTION

Legal philosophers criticize and evaluate as well as originate and expound. And their critical efforts commonly advance the subject. Indeed, critical analysis may be an avenue of progress as significant as original work itself. What are the objects and forms of criticism in legal philosophy? What evaluative standards and points of view do critics draw upon? In what ways can their criticisms 'go wrong' and for what reasons? These are large questions. Here, it is possible only to offer introductory notes of an adumbrative and programmatic character.

### II. OBJECTS AND FORMS OF CRITICISM

Objects of criticism in legal philosophy vary greatly. First, the problem that a thinker has set for himself may itself come in for criticism. Legal philosophers are interested in an immense variety of problems, including the 'nature' of law, the general functions of law, the relationships between law and morals, concepts of justice, judicial and legislative justification, the limits of law, and so on. A critic may attack another's problem as unphilosophical in nature. For example, the problem may require sociological research into, say, the actual social effects of a particular law; or it may simply be a problem of designing the appropriate legal structure or process for achieving some particular social objective; or it may come down merely to weighing the pros and cons of some specific proposal for socio-legal reform; or it may concern some peculiarity of a particular legal system. These problems, among other things, lack the kind of generality that is of philosophical interest. (This, of course, does not mean they are unimportant.)

Or a problem may be criticized as fundamentally misconceived. For example, so-called 'positivists' have addressed the question: 'In what ways are law and morals separate?' But Professor Fuller has urged that the very terms of this problem fundamentally misconceive the relevant reality: law and morals cannot be thus pulled apart—law, he says, has an 'inner morality'.[1]

The problem may 'shift around'—that is, the thinker may really be addressing himself to more than one problem without being at all clear about this. One scholar has illuminatingly shown that the so-called problem of 'legal sovereignty' really breaks down into a half dozen separate questions.[2]

The *way* the problem is *posed* may come in for criticism. Thus it may be of the objectionably vague 'what is X?' variety: What is Law? What is justice? What is morality? Or the question may 'hypostatize'—that is, it may wrongly posit an entity or entities, as for example: 'What are the criteria of valid law?' as opposed to: 'What are the criteria of valid law in legal system X?' The latter is a real problem (though not a philosophical one), whereas the former is a bogus problem. (But contrast: 'What is the nature of the criteria of valid law in legal systems generally?'[3]).

Or the problem may be formulated in tendentious terms. It may, by its very terms, suggest the appropriateness of one kind of 'answer' when the very question at issue is whether this answer, among several rivals, is the more defensible. For example, a thinker concerned to elucidate the 'apparatus for identifying the law of legal systems generally' may, instead of posing the problem in these more general and neutral terms, ask: 'What is the nature of the criteria of validity legal systems utilize to identify the rules of these systems?' Yet this way of posing the problem suggests that all law takes the form of (or is reducible to) rules, which is false, and that all issues as to what the law 'is' within legal systems may be properly represented as issues of validity, which is also false.[4]

The terms or formulations of the problem may be objectionable in another distinct way, too. Thus a problem may be posed in a way which suggests that the solution must take the form of specification of necessary and sufficient conditions or of properties

---

[1] FULLER, THE MORALITY OF LAW (2nd ed., 1969).

[2] Rees, *The Theory of Sovereignty Restated* 59 MIND 495 (1950).

[3] Cf. Wollheim, *The Nature of Law* 2 POLITICAL STUDIES 128 (1954).

[4] Professor Hart's 'rule of recognition' theory is, for example, open to these rather basic objections. See HART, THE CONCEPT OF LAW (1961).

constituting an 'essence', or the like. To cite but one example, a thinker interested in giving an account of the nature of a legal system might formulate the problem as follows: 'What are the necessary and sufficient conditions for applying the phrase "legal system" to a given society?' Yet this way of posing the problem suggests a kind of answer that would inevitably neglect important features of law, at least in some societies. Some features, while not in any rigorous sense *necessary* to the existence of law, are nonetheless *salient* features of law in many societies. Consider the notion of a Bill of Rights, or the notion of private powers to make contracts or wills. Neither is *necessary* to a system of law. Yet both are 'salient features' of some systems, and merit elucidation on that ground.

The way the problem is posed may also be objectionable because it suggests or invites the use of analytical techniques that are not appropriate. Indeed, a thinker may pose a given problem with an eye to the use of some particular technique of analysis. In legal philosophy, many so-called problems of 'definition' have been posed with an eye to the use of the technique of definition *per genus et differentiam*, a technique not always applicable.[1]

The problem itself, then, is one kind of 'object' of criticism in legal philosophy. And, as we have seen, the forms of criticism that may be directed at the problem or its formulation are highly varied in nature. But often the basic problem will not be fully stated at the outset of a piece of philosophizing about law. Indeed, it may even prove difficult to pin down a single specific problem that the author is addressing himself to. Frequently, it will seem that he is writing about a cluster of related and overlapping problems, explicit formulations of which have dropped by the way in the course of composition, displaced, as it were, by the 'solutions' the author has come up with. So, too, technique and methodology. In a piece of finished work, what the reader confronts is seldom the actual philosophizing in which method, technique, and strategy are prominent, but rather, the final results of philosophizing all tidied up and put into order.

Many of these results are called 'theories'. Thus we speak of 'theories of law', 'theories of obligation', 'theories of adjudication', 'theories of natural law', and the like. Theories may be the objects

---

[1] Cf. HART, DEFINITION AND THEORY IN JURISPRUDENCE (1953) with Hacker, *Definition in Jurisprudence* 19 THE PHILOSOPHICAL QUARTERLY 343 (1969).

of different forms of criticism. A theory may fail for want of the requisite degree of comprehensiveness. Maine, for example, criticized Austin's theory of law on the ground that it did not apply to standard examples of modern legal systems.[1] Or a theory may fail for want of conceptual adequacy. Hart, for example, has criticized Austin's theory of legal authority on the ground that the concept of a 'habit of obedience' to successive rulers cannot (conceptually speaking) account for the continuity of law-making authority in the face of a succession of rulers, inasmuch as habitual obedience to a new ruler cannot spring up overnight, nor can habits confer a 'right' or 'title' to succeed.[2]

Then, too, a theory may be internally inconsistent or incoherent. Thus Dworkin offers a criterion for distinguishing between rules and principles. Yet some of his own examples do not seem to consist with this criterion.[3]

Another kind of criticism directed at some very general theories is this: The theory may simply be wrong on its 'first-order' facts. Philosophical error can be rooted in ordinary empirical error. Thus a thinker who holds that 'habits of obedience' account for the general measure of compliance that prevails in legal systems is simply wrong on his facts and needs to have another review of the possibilities as well as the facts.[4]

Or absurd implications may be explicit in a theory. Thus, for example, Professor Fuller has offered a theory about law which commits him to saying that universities and unions have legal systems properly so called.[5] Austin held that sovereign power cannot be limited, yet this meant that his theory could not apply to the clearest cases of modern legal systems.[6] *Reductio ad absurdum* is one of the more common forms of criticism addressed to theories.

Some theories purport to elucidate some feature or features of

---

[1] MAINE, EARLY HISTORY OF INSTITUTIONS 342–400 (1888).

[2] HART, THE CONCEPT OF LAW 58 (1961).

[3] See Dworkin, *Is Law a System of Rules?* in ESSAYS IN LEGAL PHILOSOPHY 35–7 (Summers ed., 1968). Professor David Lyons has noted in conversation with me that in Dworkin's own *Riggs* v. *Palmer* example, the rule hardly functions in 'the all-or-nothing fashion' seemingly demanded by Dworkin's own theory.

[4] Cf. HART, THE CONCEPT OF LAW 198 (1961)

[5] FULLER, THE MORALITY OF LAW 124–30 (2nd ed., 1969).

[6] AUSTIN, THE PROVINCE OF JURISPRUDENCE DETERMINED 254 (Library of Ideas ed., 1954).

the conceptual framework of and about law. But here it is relevant to ask: 'Whose framework?' The layman's? That of lawyers? Of legal philosophers? Without some answer to this question we cannot know in which realm of discourse we are to test proposed theories. Laymen have only very crude concepts of law, whereas lawyers may have more refined notions. In any event, once the relevant realm of discourse is known, it becomes possible to criticize a theory on the ground that it does not really represent the relevant reality—does not really give us a true account of, say, the layman's notion of ownership, or the lawyer's idea of the nature of legal obligations, as these notions appear in the relevant realms of discourse. In a sense, such theories 'mismap' the relevant conceptual terrain.[1]

It must not be thought that just any kind of theory is interchangeably subject to just any form of criticism. Some theories may be subject to some forms of criticism that others are not, and vice versa. For example, some theories are of a very general descriptive sort while others are justificatory in nature. Obviously, theory meant only to elucidate what it is, for example, to have a legal obligation should not be criticized on the ground that this same theory does not rationally justify having systems of law in which legal obligations are recognized. Or very general justificatory theory purporting to identify the distinct grounds on which a legal system may justifiably interfere with the actions of its citizens should not be criticized as if it purported to give an account of the grounds of interference actually recognized in most systems. Descriptive and justificatory theories must not be confused.

It is possible to break most theories down into constituent elements, which can themselves be the objects of criticism, either taken alone or as parts of a more general theory. These elements include concepts, distinctions, relationships, classifications, and so on. In all of these argument, too, may figure in a variety of ways. Let's consider, briefly, some of the forms of criticism appropriate to each.

A concept (or cluster of related concepts) may be the object of

[1] Such 'mismapping' can itself take a variety of forms. In perhaps its most radical form, a theory 'mismaps' by completely 'analyzing away' the relevant concepts or cluster of concepts. For example, rather than mapping out concepts of legal duty, Kelsen analyzes them away. On this, see Woozley, *Legal Duties, Offenses and Sanctions* 77 MIND 462 (1968).

varied forms of criticism.[1] Thus a concept may not advance the elucidation at all (if elucidation be the objective). One possible reason why it may not is that it may itself be 'too close' to the phenomena that it is supposed to help elucidate. For example, Hart has noted that we should not try to elucidate the nature of legal authority by use of the notion of a command, for this notion itself involves the notion of authority.[2] Or a concept may, in a sense, be logically inappropriate, as in the example in which we said habits are not 'normative' and therefore cannot confer rights. Or a concept may be 'descriptively inapposite'. Thus a theorist may use the notion of power when what he really needs is the notion of authority, or vice versa. Or a concept may fail for want of sufficient specificity. Thus the notion of a law hides important distinctions between rules, principles, maxims, and so on. Or a concept may be misleadingly 'overextended', as in theories in which the notion of a sanction for breach of a rule is extended to cover the rather different situation of nullity for non-compliance with a rule of validation. Or a concept may, together with other concepts, be used to offer an exhaustive account of relevant phenomena yet fail in this. For example, the concepts of duty-imposing and power-conferring rules may fail to account for the basic varieties of legal rules, inasmuch as some kinds of legal rules neither confer powers nor impose duties. Concepts can fail in still other ways, too.

Distinctions, too, are often the focus of criticism in legal philosophy. Here are some rather famous distinctions that have come under fire: Bentham's distinction between law as it is and law as it ought to be; Kelsen's distinction between norms and the grundnorm; Pound's distinctions between rules, principles, concepts and standards; Hart's distinction between primary and secondary rules; Fuller's distinction between an internal and an external morality. A distinction may be criticized in many ways: for not being sharp enough—that is, for admitting cases which do not clearly fall on either side of it; for not being mutually exclu-

---

[1] Criticisms of *concepts* invoked or constructed by philosophers can frequently be restated in the form of criticisms of *terminologies* constructed or invoked by philosophers. In descriptive theories, at least, the philosopher is usually seeking a terminology in which to 'represent' or 'express' the relevant reality. But it is best here to eschew 'terminology' and utilize 'concept'. Talk of 'terminology' tends to mislead some readers into thinking that legal philosophy is merely a matter of words.          [2] HART, THE CONCEPT OF LAW 20 (1961).

sive—that is, for admitting cases which clearly fall on both sides of it; for not being exhaustive—that is, for failing to provide for all the cases it *purports* to deal with; for being too sharp—that is, for failing to cater for, say, the 'overlapping' character of the relevant reality; for being 'misdrawn'—that is, for fixing the criterion of differentiation along a line that is simply inaccurate; for relying on a singular criterion of differentiation when in fact multiple criteria are more faithful to the relevant reality; for utilizing a criterion or criteria more appropriate to a distinction of degree when the facts concern a distinction in kind, and vice versa; for being confused in some way, e.g., for confusing distinguishing marks with consequences or effects thereof; for being insignificant or trivial—as in the phrase 'a distinction without a difference'.

Again, distinctions are of different kinds. Thus we may distinguish between distinctions which are more or less 'real'—there already and awaiting discovery and articulation, as opposed to those that are in some sense 'constructed' as part of a heuristic scheme designed for study of the relevant phenomena, e.g., Hohfeld's set of distinctions between jural relations. Then we may distinguish between distinctions which are 'empirical' and distinctions which are in some sense 'logical'. For instance, it has recently been alleged that rules and principles are of a conceptually (logically) different order,[1] each with its own distinctive and peculiarly appropriate vocabulary of adjacent terminology. For example, it is said that rules apply in 'all-or-nothing fashion', whereas principles may be 'outweighed'. Rules can have 'exceptions', but not principles, and so on. Then there are very general distinctions which are formulated in the law as distinctions of *policy*. These distinctions, e.g., those which attach different degrees of culpability to reckless, purposeful and negligent conduct, are obviously more than merely 'empirical distinctions' and yet they are of a different order, too, from so-called logical distinctions.

It should be plain that not all distinctions are interchangeably subject to the same forms of criticism. Thus it would be absurd to argue against a *logical* distinction solely on grounds of policy, or to urge that heuristic distinctions which do not purport to describe the facts are factually inaccurate.

[1] See Dworkin, *Is Law a System of Rules?* in ESSAYS IN LEGAL PHILOSOPHY 37 (Summers ed., 1968).

Relationships, too, are commonly objects of criticism in legal philosophy. Legal philosophers have occasion to consider many different kinds of relationships, including logical relationships of presupposition, implication and entailment; conceptual relationships of, say, implication and co-relativity; empirical relationships of co-incidental regularity, cause and effect, concomitance, and statistical correlation; relationships of subordination, as in the phrase 'primary and secondary rules'; functional relationships, e.g., 'rules conferring private powers enabling persons to make contracts'; means-end relationships; relationships of 'existential interdependence', e.g., 'law depends on morals and morals upon law'.

Now it is familiar enough that not all alleged relationships are of the same type, and therefore, not all subject to the same forms of criticism. It would be absurd to attack a means-end relation as if it were conceptual in character, or to attack a relationship of functional primacy on the ground of reverse historical sequence.

Arguments, as well as analytical techniques and even notions of a metaphysical character may figure in the formulation of a problem, in the resulting theories offering solutions to problems, in constituent concepts, distinctions, and relationships within a theory, too. These arguments themselves often become objects of criticism. The forms of criticism appropriate to arguments are legion. They may be equivocal, may be circular, may lack internal consistency, may be vulnerable to infinite regresses, may be factually inaccurate, may prove too much, may be formally invalid, or though formally valid, lack justificatory force, and so on.

It is one thing to subject the elements of a theory, argument and all, to criticism; it is quite another to attack the presuppositions, tacit assumptions, and starting points of theories. Yet these latter are themselves often objects of criticism in legal philosophy. Fuller, for instance, has recently attacked what he takes to be the tacit assumption of 'positivists' that 'the basic concern' of legal philosophy 'is with the question, *who* can make law?'[1]

## III. CRITICAL STANDARDS AND POINTS OF VIEW

The rational 'merits' of problems in legal philosophy vary with the nature of these problems. A philosopher may set out to present

[1] FULLER, THE MORALITY OF LAW 192 (2nd ed., 1969).

a layman's 'doctrine of intention'—how laymen actually conceive intentional behavior. But while laymen do have notions of and about intentional action, they have no general 'theories' at all or only very crude ones about, say, the structure of a legal system or the relationships, say, between the concepts of utility and justice. Here it would be absurd to invoke, as the ultimate critical standard, the conceptions of ordinary laymen. Here a more immediate kind of appeal, not to 'usage' but to the 'first-order facts', is required.[1] We are to give an adequate account of the character of, say, legal authority; or of legal validity, or of legal rules, principles, and maxims; or of legal obligations and rights. Hohfeld's analysis is hardly to be found on the lips of laymen—even those who speak prose—yet his analysis admirably differentiates a variety of *possible* senses of the word 'right'.[2] It is important to stress that first-order facts may be of very different kinds. They may concern the behavior of citizens, the psychologically possible states of mind of citizens; the behavior of judges; the kinds of reasons judges give for their opinions; the kinds of criticisms officials make of each other's actions; the kinds of rules, etc., a system lays down; the procedures legislatures follow, and so on.

Not all the ultimate critical standards in legal philosophy are reflected in the critic's appeals merely to linguistic facts or to first-order facts. The critic also appeals to what might be called criteria of conceptual adequacy. Thus 'command of the sovereign' is conceptually inadequate to account for law made by courts and law in the form of custom, as well as for constitutional law. The notion of a 'habit' cannot yield legal authority, for authority is normative and habits are not. Hart's concept of a 'rule of recognition' is conceptually too simple to represent the complex and varied law-identifying phenomena operative in modern legal systems. To cite one final example: neither the notion of a definition nor that of a mere statement of fact is conceptually adequate to characterize illuminatingly the truisms of human experience on

[1] This has long been recognized in legal philosophy. Yet at this late date Professor Fuller persists in accusing some thinkers as follows: 'In general the practice of ordinary-language philosophy consists in digging out and clarifying the distinctions embedded in everyday linguistic usage. In whatever field these distinctions are found, there seems to be a kind of presumption that they will prove valid and useful and that once they have been fully articulated there is no need to go further.' FULLER, THE MORALITY OF LAW 195–6 (2nd ed., 1969). Indeed, the late J. L. Austin did not even believe the foregoing.

[2] HOHFELD, FUNDAMENTAL LEGAL CONCEPTIONS (1919).

B

which sensible natural law theories are built. These truisms are not true by definition, yet in their truth they are 'stronger' than are ordinary true statements of fact. Some new concept—natural necessity?—is required if we are to do justice to their character.[1]

Then, too, the legal philosopher, in selecting the building blocks of a theory, will often appeal to notions of what is of fundamental social significance within any system of law—not the color of judges' gowns, nor the kind of paper that court reporters use. These cannot be *salient* features of legal systems. But what can? Perhaps the criteria of salience vary? That something like a 'rule of recognition' is a salient feature (perhaps also even a defining feature) of legal systems is so because of the socially significant role it plays in providing an apparatus for identifying the law of the system. But with law's 'minimum necessary content', also a salient feature of legal systems, the criterion of salience is significantly different, and pertains to what might be called the system's 'viability'.

Or the ultimate appeal may be to standards of clarity, consistency and coherence. Indeed, the appeal *may* even be to some model of valid inference worked up by a formal logician, for the question may be whether a *type* of argument frequently utilized in legal justifications is formally valid.

Finally (for here), the relevant critical standard may concern the appropriate level of generality. Thus if the analysis is in over-general terminology, it may obscure or mask philosophically important differences.[2] On the other hand, if the analysis descends to a lower level of generality, it may incorporate features of the phenomena that are merely peculiar to the legal system at hand and of no real philosophical interest.

Substantive critical *standards* to which legal philosophers appeal, then, are remarkably varied in nature, and include: linguistic facts; first-order facts; criteria of conceptual adequacy; considerations of fundamental social significance; notions of consistency, clarity, coherence, and logical validity; and relevant levels of analysis.

What, though, of critical *points of view*?[3] These are not the same

---

[1] Cf. HART, THE CONCEPT OF LAW 195 (1961).

[2] Cf. Hart's criticisms in terms of 'this is . . . no more than a convenient shorthand for complex facts which still await description', and 'these blanket terms . . . merely mask vital differences'. HART, THE CONCEPT OF LAW 110–12 (1961).

[3] On points of view, see Moline, *On Points of View* 5 AMERICAN PHILOSOPHICAL QUARTERLY 191 (1968). And cf. URMSON, THE EMOTIVE THEORY OF ETHICS, Ch. 9 (1968).

as critical standards. And critical points of view figure prominently in legal philosophy. A problem, a theory, a concept, an argument, may be distinctively evaluated by reference to a point of view. Thus, a critic may claim that a given piece of work neglects a point of view and thus distorts the relevant reality. To cite examples: Some theorists have confused legal with moral duty. In criticizing their theories, Holmes stressed that we should look at law and morals from the 'point of view of a bad man' who is concerned to keep the law, or if not to keep it, at least to count the material costs. To this bad man, the distinction between legal and moral duty will, so Holmes thought, appear clear and striking.[1]

Hart has criticized so-called 'predictive' theories of law for their failure to take account of what he calls the 'internal point of view' of citizens and officials toward the laws to which they are subject:[2]

What the external point of view, which limits itself to the observable regularities of behaviour, cannot reproduce is the way in which the rules function as rules in the lives of those who normally are the majority of society. These are the officials, lawyers, or private persons who use them, in one situation after another, as guides to the conduct of social life, as the basis for claims, demands, admissions, criticism, or punishment, viz., in all the familiar transactions of life according to rules. For them the violation of a rule is not merely a basis for the prediction that a hostile reaction will follow but a *reason* for hostility.

But just as distortion can flow from neglect or failure to take account of a point of view and its own criteria of relevance, so too, distortion can flow from 'over-fixing' on a given point of view. For example, Fuller has recently condemned those thinkers who adopt a 'managerial' point of view towards law and thus neglect the 'relatively stable reciprocity of expectations between law giver and subject [which] is part of the very idea of a functioning legal order'.[3]

It must not be assumed that for any and all work in legal philosophy there already exists ready to hand relevant critical standards and critical points of view by which this work may be judged. On this, more later.

---

[1] Holmes, *The Path of the Law* 10 HARVARD LAW REVIEW 457 (1897).

[2] HART, THE CONCEPT OF LAW 88 (1961).

[2] FULLER, THE MORALITY OF LAW 209 (2nd ed., 1969). For a criticism that Fuller 'overfixes' on a 'legislative point of view' and thereby distorts, see my own paper in this collection.

### IV. CRITICISM OF CRITICISM

Criticism in legal philosophy, as in any subject, can go wrong in a variety or ways, and thus itself be subject to a variety of forms of criticism. It remains to inventory some of these forms of criticism and to suggest some reasons why critical work goes wrong in these ways.

First, much criticism rests on misinterpretation and is therefore irrelevant. In legal philosophy misinterpretation is endemic. Examples are legion. But why? Perhaps it is partly because in this subject (more than most) nearly everyone has an axe of his own to grind and he wants to get on with that. And the subject is complex and difficult—where this is so there is always special scope for misinterpretation. Then there are persons working in the field who represent very different backgrounds and traditions. Some are philosophers as such. Some are mainly lawyers. Some are both. Some are neither. This diversity injects distinctive risks of non-communication. Thus, for example, some academic lawyers are prone to read an author's prose as if it appeared in a statute or a will. Yet the ideal reader should read some authors in legal philosophy—Fuller is a good example—not so much for their efforts at detailed analytical development of specific points, but rather for the suggestive drift or gist of what they have to say. Then I suspect a tendency to pigeon-hole and categorize thinkers and theories in terms of the traditional 'schools of jurisprudence' frequently gets in the way. We tend too often to read not for what a thinker is saying but for whom, among several 'schools' proto-types, he sounds most like. While this is a kind of short-cut, it is not a short-cut to understanding. Sometimes stubbornness gets in the way, too, just as in most subjects.[1]

Second, assuming the critic has properly resolved initial issues of interpretation, issues of 'characterization' may still remain. And if he fails to resolve these as he should, what he says will prove irrelevant (though in a different sense). One of the more common 'characterization' questions is this: 'Is the author making a

---

[1] Again, Professor Fuller continues to want to find doctrinal unity—'school-like unity'—in the work of those I once called 'The New Analytical Jurists' (a designation with which he has much fun). See FULLER, THE MORALITY OF LAW 191 (2nd ed., 1969). But my own protestations and arguments precisely to the contrary, he remarks that I 'seem throughout to have some difficulty in articulating just what philosophic creed unites this new school of thought'.

philosophical point, or is he merely talking law?' One of the most spectacular mischaracterizations in these terms to appear in recent literature is described below:[1]

I must, however, draw attention here to the fact that most of Professor Bodenheimer's misquotations or misunderstandings of what I said seem to spring from a single pervasive error of considerable importance; it is indeed one which has been recognized by contemporary philosophers as a source of confusion in many different fields. It is this: Professor Bodenheimer either cannot distinguish or thinks it of no importance to distinguish between, on the one hand, *law* and *legal concepts* and, on the other, *theories* of or about law, and *definitions* of legal concepts. So he makes me look *sillier* than I hope I am, by treating the observations which I in fact make about legal *theories* and about the character of *definitions* of legal concepts as if these observations had been made about *law* and *legal concepts* themselves. Thus, to take one example, he quotes me as saying of legal concepts such as that of a corporate body that *they* 'tend to have their heads in the clouds' whereas I had in fact said that *theories* concerning the nature of corporate entities 'seem to the lawyer to stand apart with their heads at least in the clouds' precisely because the actual use in a legal system of such legal concepts 'can be reconciled with any theory but is authority for none'.

But even once the basic enterprise is characterized as philosophical, other more particular misconstruals may occur along the way which not uncommonly nullify critical effort. Misconstrual is all the more likely when court cases are cited, for this always invites someone to do a bit of legal analysis. For example, when Dworkin referred to court cases as illustrating particular legal principles, it was not necessary to his argument that the judges *in these cases* saw themselves to be or were in fact using these principles to alter clearly applicable 'pre-existing rules'. Thus Christie's lengthy *legal analysis* designed to show that these cases did not involve such rules was certainly indecisive and probably irrelevant.[2] What Dworkin needed to show was that legal rules and legal principles are different. Now it may be that Dworkin had the wrong notion of a legal rule. But no amount of legal analysis of two cases would ever show that.

Third, the critic may go awry simply by invoking the wrong

---

[1] Hart, *Analytical Jurisprudence in Mid-Twentieth Century: A Reply to Professor Bodenheimer*, 105 U. PENNSYLVANIA LAW REVIEW 954 (1957).
[2] See Christie, *The Model of Principles* 1968 DUKE LAW JOURNAL 649.

critical standards or critical points of view. And obviously this can render his criticism entirely nugatory. Thus, for example, many thinkers have sought to formulate criteria for evaluating the reasoning in judicial opinions. Frequently these criteria have been criticized for incorporating or, indeed, for not incorporating notions of formal validity from the discipline of formal logic.[1] Yet all such criticisms are null and void if it is in fact the case that formal logic is a fundamentally irrelevant source of standards for evaluating what is truly significant in judicial reasoning.

Legal philosophers offer analyses of concepts in terms of elements or features, and much criticism in legal philosophy is directed at these analyses. A form of criticism that is still all too common is that one or more of the analyst's 'elements' or 'features' are not always present in every instance of the application of the relevant phrase or word. Yet this kind of critical argument by way of counter-example often misconceives the relevant conceptual reality, for it is often true that it is not possible to specify a discrete set of elements or features that are always present in this way. By now, this is almost a truism.

Theoretical inquiries about law or a legal concept are often confused with inquiries into the best way for law or a legal process to function if it is to maximize utility or achieve justice. This confusion, in turn, can result in confusion of the relevant critical standards. For example, how judges ought to interpret statutes is one thing, but the general practices they do follow in interpreting statutes may be quite another. Failure of a critic to observe this distinction can lead him to criticize a theoretical account of interpretational practices *as if* this account were offered as a recommendation on how judges ought to interpret statutes.[2]

One further famous example: Professors Hart and Fuller have been doing battle for over a decade now, and Fuller has only recently fired another vast volley.[3] Yet *much* of what each has written ostensibly in criticism of the other's work often seems to miss the mark. Could it be that they have basically different interests—basically different points of view toward law—interests

---

[1] I once got it all badly wrong. *Don't see* Summers, *Logic in the Law* 72 MIND 254 (1963).

[2] A well-known example is Fuller, *Positivism & Fidelity to Law—A Reply to Professor Hart* 71 HARVARD LAW REVIEW 661–9 (1958).

[3] And in which one finds much insight. See the new chapter *A Reply to My Critics* in FULLER, THE MORALITY OF LAW 187–224 (2nd ed., 1969).

and points of view which are really in the main, logically quite compatible? It is really no criticism to evaluate another's work by standards he does not intend, at least when that work itself does not intrinsically invite evaluation by these standards. Take, for example, Fuller's criticism of Hart's work on the structure of legal systems. Or Hart's criticism of Fuller's work on the concept of purpose in law. These are at bottom basically different (and compatible) interests. Yet often each critic proceeds as if these interests, and the correspondingly applicable evaluative standards, were the same. Yet these are not the same, and this means, among other things, that the critics have to be willing, if they are going to criticize, to meet each other *more* on each other's respective home grounds. For example, Fuller would have to learn a bit more analytic philosophy, and Hart some Hegel?

## V. WHITHER?

One picture is this: a piece of work is done; it is then judged by reference to pre-existing and well-defined critical standards and points of view; it is judged up or judged down. Now, this picture does tell some of the story. But it tells far from the whole of the story. For often in legal philosophy, it is not like this.

For one thing, relatively new work is being done all the time. To the extent this new work is on relatively new questions, the articulation and refinement of at least some of the relevant critical standards and points of view has to await progress on the basic questions themselves. Obviously we cannot know how to criticize until we understand what is going on, and even then, with novel work, we may not immediately see what we should say about it. And it might just turn out that the relevant test is whether the work casts light, rather than whether it measures up against a well-defined critical standard or point of view.

Then, in the course of some kinds of work, issues may arise which are, so to speak, undecidable. Suppose, for example, that the issue is how, in common usage, we distinguish between 'obligations' and 'duties'. Upon investigation, it might transpire that there are no stable and consistently applied forms of usage here. In this event, we might say the issue was not really decidable.

Or, to cite a second example, suppose a thinker wishes to preserve a distinction between law and morals, yet wants to insist that judges are bound not only to apply rules but also to apply certain broad moral principles, at least in those cases where rules do not control. He will then have to face the question whether he can formulate a criterion for differentiating those moral principles that are law from those that are not. He might quite naturally hypothesize that special forms of criticism are directed at a judge when he fails to apply moral principles that are also law. Yet, on inquiry, he might find this is not so, and that essentially the same criticisms are made for failure to apply a relevant moral principle whether or not that principle is already in some sense law. And upon further inquiry, he might be led to conclude that there just is no satisfactory general criterion for differentiating legal from non-legal moral principles. He might have to say that it just is a fact that as of a given time in a particular legal system, certain moral principles are law and certain ones are not. (In philosophy, as in other subjects, we sometimes want more than the relevant reality will let us have.)

Or, undecidability may flow from the character of the analytical apparatus that a thinker is using. Thus the issue may arise whether, say, sanctions are merely a salient feature of modern legal systems or are, rather, more fundamental and therefore a defining feature also. But this issue may not prove readily decidable, not because it is especially difficult, but because the distinction between defining features and salient features is not itself one which can be readily applied to all important cases.

To conclude: Criticism is an important avenue of progress in legal philosophy. Critical analysis takes many forms, and we would no doubt do well to sharpen our awareness of the critical frameworks and devices we utilize.[1] This paper is a modest contribution to that effort. It is inevitably adumbrative and programmatic. A careful study of the five 'critical' assessments in this volume will reveal that much more remains to be said, both by way of refinement and extension.

---

[1] Cf. Cavell, *Austin at Criticism* in SYMPOSIUM ON J. L. AUSTIN 71 (Fann ed., 1969) where it is said: 'I cannot attempt to complete the list of Austin's terms of criticism, any more than I can now attempt to trace the particular target each of them has . . . Austin often gives no reasons whatever for thinking one or the other of them true . . . according to anything like the standards he imposes on his own constructions . . . This discrepancy is not, I believe, peculiar to Austin . . . [M]y feeling is that if it could be understood here, one would understand something about the real limitations, or liabilities, of the exercise of philosophy.'

But it must not be assumed that comprehensive systematic analysis of our critical apparatus is either possible (at any given point in time) or would tell all. Some important questions have not even been thought about (no doubt). And some are likely to prove undecidable. Then, too, there remains the relatively unexplored domain of strategy and tactics, not of the critic but of the original thinker. His hope is to cast some light. Often his success will depend on whether he can devise a relevant technique, analytical apparatus, or framework. But this is likely to be highly 'question-bound' (and 'thinker-bound'?). Perhaps it is, therefore, best left relatively unexplored. Creative processes cannot be formalized.

# Bentham, Lecture on a Master Mind

## H. L. A. HART*

In 1838 when John Stuart Mill wrote his famous essay on Bentham,[1] Bowring's edition of Bentham's works, which included much not previously published, was still in progress. Mill says that at this time 'except for the more slight of his works' Bentham's readers had been few. It seems that the completion in 1843 of the Bowring edition did not vastly increase their numbers. In 1864 Richard Hildreth, an American lawyer and moralist, embarked on the strange project of translating back from French into English Dumont's very free version of some of Bentham's writings on the Principles of Legislation. Hildreth tells us in the preface to his translation that he was inspired to publish it because, in spite of their fame abroad, Bentham's works 'in England and America, though frequently spoken of, are little read'. This is still true; and a very great proportion of Bentham's published work has for long been relegated to an intellectual lumber room visited only by the historian. It is clear that the discouraging close print and double columns of the Bowring edition are not solely responsible for this. Even when the new and splendid edition to be published by the Athlone Press of the University of London becomes available, the reading of the largely unread Bentham will not prove easy. The difficulties are well known: so many of the major controversies to which his writings relate are dead or transformed; so many of the reforms demanded in the name of Utility have long been conceded; often only an historian with a detailed knowledge of

* Professor of Jurisprudence in the University of Oxford 1953–69; Fellow of University College, Oxford. The essay which appears here first appeared in 48 PROCEEDINGS OF THE BRITISH ACADEMY 297 (1962) and is reprinted here with the kind permission of the author, the British Academy, and the Oxford University Press.

[1] DISSERTATIONS AND DISCUSSIONS, Vol. I, pp. 330–92. 'Bentham' first published in the LONDON AND WESTMINSTER REVIEW (1938)

the period could judge how far the Benthamite reforms which were not adopted would have been an improvement and what the total effect was of those reforms which were adopted. There is, moreover, along with the diverting wit and splendid invective, much eccentric and exasperating pedantry in Bentham's later style with its proliferation of invented 'Greek-sprung' technical terms and his exploration in infinite detail of every project.

Nonetheless, the legend of Bentham's unreadability is disturbing and it is worth attempting an amateur estimate of the amount of Bentham's published work which is, in fact, read at the present time. For most readers without a very specialized interest, Bentham's thought is represented by the *Fragment of Government* and the *Principles of Morals and Legislation*. These are easily accessible in modern editions, and are the only works of Bentham's which could be described as widely read and which at the present time enter regularly, though (*crede experto*) by no means in their entirety, into the academic teaching of political philosophy or politics or jurisprudence. The specialist in the philosophy of law—a small enough class in this country—reads the two brilliant works discovered by Mr. Charles Everett among the Bentham folios: *The Comment on the Commentaries*[1] and *The Limits of Jurisprudence Defined.*[2] Mr. C. K. Ogden's book, published in 1933 on Bentham's *Theory of Fictions* with its collection of passages from the essays on Logic, Ontology, and Universal Grammar, brought to the notice of philosophers, in most cases almost certainly for the first time, the fact that Bentham had anticipated by a century part of Bertrand Russell's doctrine on logical constructions and incomplete symbols. That doctrine, at the time of Mr. Ogden's publication, was looked upon by many English and American philosophers as the paradigm of philosophical method and the prime solvent of philosophical perplexities. Finally, Dr. Starks's recent three-volume anthology[3] of the economic writings, much of which had not been previously published, has done something to show to economists the range and power of Bentham's thought on monetary theory, investment, and employment. It is clear that there is cause to question Lord Keynes's judgment that 'Bentham was not an economist at all'.[4]

[1] Oxford: Clarendon Press, 1928.   [2] Columbia University Press, 1935.
[3] Allen & Unwin for the Royal Economic Society (London, 1952).
[4] THE END OF LAISSEZ-FAIRE, p. 19.

Quantitatively the works I have mentioned constitute a tiny fragment of the whole. They amount together to about 750,000 words. But the Bowring edition alone, if we exclude the last two volumes (which are occupied with correspondence and biography), must on a conservative estimate contain about 5 million words and it is by no means the whole of what will appear in the new edition now planned. How far does this matter? Do the few works which are commonly read and lectured upon or discussed in universities and elsewhere represent adequately all that is still of living speculative interest in the product of Bentham's mind? Is it true that the rest for all its bulk and diversity of subject-matter is only of historical interest? Constitutional Code, Education, Model Prison, Legislative Procedure, The Law of Evidence, Usury, Taxation, Declarations of Rights—is it true that all this is mere application and painful elaboration in detail of the few principles which can be adequately understood from the few works that are still constantly read? John Stuart Mill's essay may, I think, have done something to spread the impression that this must be so. For in his assessment of Bentham's qualities Mill asserts that the novelty and value of what he did 'lay not in his opinions but in his method' which Mill described as the 'method of detail'. My own view which I shall shortly attempt to substantiate is that this is a misleading dichotomy between opinions and methods. Methods sufficiently novel, as some of Bentham's were, cannot be mere innovations of method. They presuppose too fundamental a reorientation of the direction of inquiry, and too radical a shift in the conception of what is to be considered an acceptable answer. We are too often forced to the conclusion that Bentham has provided us with a new question, rather than merely a new answer, for his innovation to be considered matters of method alone.

Mill says that Bentham's novelty of method lay in his remorseless insistence on the criticism of existing law and institutions, and in his schemes of reform on 'treating wholes by breaking them down into parts, abstraction by resolving them into things and generalizations by distinguishing them into the individuals of which they are made up'. These are of course among the habits of thought and the modes of investigation of the scientist, and it may well be thought that when they are used in the application of the principles of Utility to such subjects as the Panopticon prison, or the reform of the Poor Law or the Court of Chancery, nothing of lasting speculative importance is likely to emerge. Haphazard experimentation with what I shall call (of course inaccurately) the unread Bentham, is apt to confirm this impression. A *sors Benthamiana* made with the finger at random is likely to bring to light a passage prescribing, perhaps, the precise shape and size of the beds or the form of central heating to be used in prisons, or the clothes or even the bedding to be used in workhouses. The following passage on the paupers' bedding perhaps conveys the flavour sufficiently well:

Beds stuffed with straw: one side covered with the cheapest linen or hempen cloth for summer; the other with coarse woollen cloth for winter. Stretching the under sheet on hooks pins or buttons will save the quantity usually added for tucking in. In cold weather that the woollen may be in contact with the body the sheet might be omitted. A rug and two blankets and an upper sheet to be of no greater width than the cell and to be tacked on to one of the blankets. . . . Straw, the more frequently changed the better particularly in warm months. To the extent of the quantity wanted for littering cattle, the change will cost nothing, and beyond that quantity the expense will only be the difference between the value of the straw as straw and the value of it as manure.[1]

It is perhaps difficult when immersed in this—or indeed sunk in it—to remember that this is a philosopher writing; but two things should prevent our forgetting it. The first is that embedded even in this kind of detail there are bold and provocative reaffirmations of the general principles which gain in clarity and in a sense reveal more of their meaning when applied to small things. Thus only eight pages before this disquisition on bedding there is a discussion of 'the only shape which genuine and efficient humanity [in dealing with the indigent poor] can take'.[2] As in the state so in the poor house 'the duty-and-interest-juncture-principle' is to be applied so that throughout it shall be in the interests of the managers to look after those in their care. The salaries of the governor are to be reduced for every woman who dies in childbirth and to vary with the number of juvenile inmates who survive from year to year. Extra premiums and bounties are to be awarded for less than average mortality. Why so? Because, says Bentham,

[1] OUTLINE OF PAUPER MANAGEMENT IMPROVED 389 (Bowring ed., Vol. III) first published in Young's ANNALS OF AGRICULTURE, 1797.    [2] op. cit., p. 381.

every system of management which has disinterestedness pretended or real for its foundation is rotten at the root, susceptible of a momentary prosperity at the outset but sure to perish in the long run. That priniciple of action is most to be depended upon whose influence is most powerful, most constant, most uniform, most lasting and most general among mankind. Personal interest is that principle and a system of economy built on any other foundation is built upon a quicksand.[1]

A study of the duty-and-interest-juncture-principle thus applied by Bentham as early as 1797 to the microcosm of the poor-house would correct many errors in the interpretation of Bentham's radicalism. It would kill the common theory that to the objection that on his principles there was no reason why the legislator should make such laws as would secure the greatest happiness of the greatest number, Bentham could only reply by making the assumption that the legislator was a person who *happened* to find his own happiness in promoting that of others.[2]

But, secondly, the extraordinary combination in Bentham of a fly's-eye view of practical detail with boldness or even rashness in generalization, especially about human nature, is of more than psychological interest. It was part of the intellectual tactics if not the strategy of the campaign for reform. It was said by Bentham's critics that he believed mistakenly that if he could articulate to the last detail the application of a general theory, he believed that this showed the theory to be sound.[3] This interesting criticism is, I think, false; what is, however, true is that he thought the criticism of existing institutions unaccompanied by demonstrably practical alternatives was worthless; and he believed this not only because

---

[1] ibid.

[2] Some ambiguity in the expression 'legislator' (as between the framer of an ideal Benthamite Constitution and those possessing legislative authority in actual governments) may have befogged the issue. See A. J. Ayer in JEREMY BENTHAM AND THE LAW 213 (London, 1948), where Bentham is said to have made this assumption about the 'lawgiver' or 'legislator'. Professor Ayer cites in support the Introduction to the CONSTITUTIONAL CODE 7 (Bowring ed., Vol. IX) but here Bentham merely says that the only reason why he himself desires that form of government to be adopted, which would bring about the greatest happiness of the greatest number, is that this would be 'in the highest degree contributory to my own greatest happiness'. He does not assume that this is true of the rulers of any society; their interest must be *made* to coincide with the universal interest by the institution of representative democracy and the other applications of the 'duty-and-interest-juncture-principle' enjoined in Bentham's Constitutional Code.

[3] LESLIE STEPHEN, THE ENGLISH UTILITARIANS, Vol. I, p. 283.

criticism, like everything else, was to be judged by its Utility, but because hatred of anarchy and disorder was as strong a passion with him as hatred of blind custom and conservatism. For all his vehemence against the oppressors of his day and their abettors the judges and lawyers, his advice was 'To obey punctually; to censure freely'[1] until a sober calculation in terms of utility showed a clear profit in disobedience. But to criticize and destroy *without* a clear conception of what was to follow was, for Bentham, the mark of the anarchical spirit, and the now tiresome blueprints with their forests of detail did more than manifest Bentham's strange temperament. They were intended to be a demonstration that a middle path between conservatism and anarchy was possible, and this was itself to destroy the neurotic fear of innovation which was one of the major obstacles to reform.

## II

Still the question remains: What sort of speculative interest remains now to be extracted from the vast unread areas of Bentham? Will better acquaintance with them widen the scope of the discussion of his ideas which has for very many years been confined to a very few topics expounded in relatively few of Bentham's pages? For the topics have been few as well as the pages. In this century little of Bentham's thought has been regularly expounded, discussed, and criticized apart from the philosophical and pyschological doctrines of utility which concern the relation of pain and pleasure to desire and action on the one hand, and to morality and the criticism of social institutions on the other. So it is, I think fair to say, that Bentham has become almost exclusively a text (often indeed displaced by Mill's *Essay on Utilitarianism*) for the debate of a few questions regarded of prime importance in the teaching of moral philosophy. Is all desire for pleasure or the avoidance of pain? Is it possible to compare the pleasures and pains of different persons? Is moral arithmetic, that is a calculus of pleasures and pains, intelligible and if intelligible is it applicable to all or only some types of moral issues or questions of legislative choice? Can Justice be accommodated within an analysis of all moral ideas in terms of Utility as merely the most efficient means of distributing pain or pleasure? Or can one accommodate it and

---

[1] A FRAGMENT ON GOVERNMENT, Preface para. 16, p. 230 (Bowring ed., Vol. I).

other apparently recalcitrant moral notions with the aid of the refinement—or device—known as 'restricted utilitarianism' at which Bentham himself at least hinted[1] and which treats Utility not as the criterion of particular actions but of general rules and social institutions?

All these are of course immensely important questions in philosophy and with major changes in the general tone and temper of the philosophy of mind such as have taken place in the past thirty years, new life has been given to them. Thus, for example, in the light of the new understanding of the concept of pleasure which has been gained largely from a more detailed and philosophically more sensitive scrutiny of the vast diversity of the *idioms* of pleasure it seems no longer possible to treat pleasure, as Bentham for the most part does, as always the name of an identifiable sensation[2] having the modalities of intensity and duration and the other 'dimensions' which he attributes to it. Nor is it possible to differentiate between the different kinds of pleasure as Bentham appears to do, that is by distinguishing the different *causes* which produce the identifiable sensation of pleasure. It is of course true that we take pleasure in eating or drinking; that we

[1] e.g., in his explanation of the binding force of alienations of property and contracts. See PRINCIPLES OF CIVIL CODE 332 (Bowring ed., Vol. I).

[2] Interpretations of Bentham's concept of pleasure have sometimes been given which divorce it from sensation or even enjoyment. Thus Burton in his Introduction to the Bowring edition (Vol. I, pp. 22 et seq.) claimed that 'the term nearest to being synonymous with pleasure [in Bentham] is volition. What it pleases a man to do is simply what he wills to do'. Though this resembles some modern analyses of pleasure there are formidable objections to it as an interpretation of Bentham: (1) Bentham frequently refers to pleasures as sensations, e.g. in the PRINCIPLES OF MORALS AND LEGISLATION, Ch. IV, ss. 5 and 6, and most strikingly the manuscripts published as Appendixes 4 and 5 in Baumgardt's BENTHAM AND THE ETHICS OF TODAY (Princeton Univ. Press, 1952) especially pp. 556, 557 and 577. (2) Bentham gave fifty-eight synonyms for pleasure including in them 'enjoyment' but not 'volition', 'choice', or 'preference' or any cognate idea (See TABLE OF THE SPRINGS OF ACTION 205, Bowring ed., Vol. I). The idea of pleasure is said to 'apply itself' to the will and to have as its 'effects' or 'consequences' *velleity, volition,* and *action* (op. cit., p. 209). (3) For Bentham pleasure and pain are 'real entities' whereas *all* other psychological entities including volition are 'fictions' (op. cit., p. 211, and Bowring, Vol. VIII, pp. 207–8). Pleasure and pain are said to be 'susceptible of existence' without the rest and 'as often as they come unlooked for do actually come into existence' without them (Bowring, Vol. I, p. 211).

Notwithstanding these objections it is certainly arguable that Bentham did not think of the connection between voluntary action and pleasure as merely contingent. But if he did not, it seems likely that he thought 'volition' definable in terms of pleasure and pain rather than vice versa.

enjoy a walk; that we are pleased with a child's progress, or by someone's good fortune, or at the news of an inheritance, or of Hitler's defeat. These are examples of what Bentham describes as the pleasure of sense, of property, of expectation, and so on. But nothing but an obstinate loyalty to the philosophy of mind of the eighteenth century could make us say that these are all cases where a sensation of pleasure occurs and is produced by so many different causes. What we *do* mean by referring to these as cases of pleasure has, no doubt, not yet been exhaustively or even sufficiently explained. But the outlines at least of a new and more realistic analysis are clear. The elements previously treated as mere empirical evidence of a separately identifiable sensation of pleasure have now been introduced into the analysis of pleasure.[1] The wish for prolongation of the activity or experience enjoyed; the resistance to interruption; the absorbed or rapt attention; the absence of some further end beyond the activity enjoyed—these are surely conceptually and not merely empirically linked with pleasure, and this revision in analysis must call for a restatement of the propositions of psychological hedonism and so for a fresh criticism of them. For the proposition that all desire is for pleasure (or the avoidance of pain) has now lost its simple outline which depended on treating pleasure as always some sensation caused by our activities: and it was this which made the idea appear easily intelligible even if it was empirically false.

Similarly, the idea of a calculus of pleasures and pains must be reinterpreted in the light of a different and, I should say, better understanding of the concepts of pain and pleasure, if only because it seems clear that they do not have the logical symmetry which Bentham ascribes to them. But it is by no means clear that Bentham will, on all points, be the loser by this process of reinterpretation; on some points the wheel will perhaps be seen to come full circle. Thus thirty years ago both philosophers and economists of repute said and indeed wrote that it was logically impossible, not merely difficult, in fact to compare one man's pleasure or satisfaction with another's.[2] On this view, assertions that a starving man

---

[1] See T. Penelhum, *The Logic of Pleasure* PHILOSOPHY AND PHENOMENOLOGICAL RESEARCH 488 (1957); G. Ryle and W. B. Gallie, *Pleasure* PROCEEDINGS OF THE ARISTOTELIAN SOCIETY 135 (Suppl. Vol. 28, 1954); B. A. Williams and E. Bedford, *Pleasure and Belief* ibid. 57 (Suppl. Vol 33, 1959).

[2] ROBBINS, THE NATURE AND SIGNIFICANCE OF ECONOMIC SCIENCE pp. 138 ff. (London, 1937).

gets more satisfaction than a rich man from a loaf of bread or an extra £1 could never rank as a statement of fact though this status *was* allowed to an individual's comparisons between his own satisfactions as when he says that he got more pleasure from his breakfast than from his lunch. On this theory, dominant thirty years ago and perhaps still flourishing in some quarters, interpersonal comparisons of the intensity of pleasures or satisfactions were nothing but disguised value judgments of a non-utilitarian kind. They expressed the moral or conventional judgments that it was better to give the loaf to the starving man than to the rich man, better, not because it gave more pleasure or satisfaction or happiness but simply because it was 'in itself' better. This sceptical doctrine which would equally deny the status of factual statement to the assertion that one man was more angry or more frightened than another is now exceedingly difficult to sustain, whatever other objections there may be to Bentham's moral arithmetic. For it seems to depend on two dogmas: the first was that the intensity of pleasure is the intensity of a pure sensation; the second was that while the intensity of such sensations could be experienced by and so known to the subject, it could never be known or even inferred with reasonable certainty by others. Both these ideas seem now mistaken, and the second only to be acceptable as part of a total scepticism about the very existence of 'other persons' minds and feelings' which those who held that interpersonal comparisons were value judgments certainly did not intend to espouse. It may well be that for the purposes of an economic metric there were, and are, many good reasons for shifting from talk of satisfactions to 'indifference curves' or 'revealed preferences'. Such comparisons as we can make between different persons' pleasures are no doubt often too crude for the economist's purposes and may be useless to him unless we can not only compare the intensity of different persons' pleasures but *measure* the differences and say by how much one exceeds the other. Nonetheless, the old epistemological arguments against Bentham's doctrine seem wrong. His doctrine needs to be weighed again with the new weights provided by a different understanding of his fundamental concepts of pain and pleasure and the logical relation between them and their manifestations.

## III

So though, as I have claimed, the proportion of Bentham's writings that are still texts for discussion is a tiny one, their importance is still very great and their vitality seems to be inextinguishable. I doubt, however, that on these central traditional Benthamite themes very much new light will be thrown as more of his work becomes physically more readable and in fact more read. It is rather a question of deciding what we shall say on these old themes when we look at them afresh through the framework of a new philosophy. I am, however, sure that there are buried amid the detail of the less-read works, new topics which ought to be added to the discussion and I shall devote the rest of this lecture to some examples of these which are pertinent to the disciplines of law and philosophy on which alone I have any right to speak.

I have already said that Bentham was as much inspired by hatred of anarchy and revolution as he was by hatred of the apologist for the established order and the worship, as he called it, of 'dead men's bones'. Now Bentham thought in a wholly original way of these two sets of adversaries blocking the path of rational criticism and reform. This is hardly represented in the few texts of his which are regularly discussed. For he thought of them as both equipped with poisoned weapons[1] for blinding men to their real interests and making them, on the one hand, submissive to tyranny and the oppression of the many by the few and, on the other, prone to insurrection and violence. These poisoned weapons were, in a sense, intellectual ones and are vastly heterogeneous. Some of them were old and false saws or fallacious maxims repeated so often and handed down so long that they have acquired a spurious patina of sanctity. Bentham thought that they stood in the path of the rational criticism of law and social institutions, just as the maxims of scholastic philosophy, wrongly held to be both universally applicable and self-evidently true, stood in the way of progress in the natural sciences:[2] as if, to take a modern example, Darwin's evolutionary theory with its supporting evidence had been met with some hoary causal maxim of the Middle Ages such as 'The less cannot produce the greater' (*'Minus nequit gignere plus'*).

---

[1] THE BOOK OF FALLACIES 486 (Bowring ed., Vol. II).
[2] A FRAGMENT OF GOVERNMENT, Preface, para 24, n. 2.

A great many of these stale shibboleths of reaction are collected, criticized, and exploded in Bentham's vastly entertaining *Book of Fallacies* which was conceived by him as an assault on the rhetoric of despotism. The general neglect of this work in the teaching of political theory seems to me strange;[1] for it is as readable and entertaining as it is instructive and it is full of contemporary relevance. Here are dissected The Chinese Argument or the argument from the Wisdom of Our Ancestors; The Hobgoblin Argument or 'No Innovation'; the argument called the Official Malefactors' Screen with its slogan, still used, 'Attack us and you Attack all Government'. Here, too, is 'Non Causa pro Causa', by which the cause of progress and obstacles to it are confounded: as when the influence of the Crown and the presence of Bishops in the House of Lords are represented as the cause of good government, or the education provided at Oxford and Cambridge as the causes of the spread of useful national learning. Yet for all their importance fallacies of this sort were not the most dangerous poisoned weapons in the armoury of reaction nor did their identification and exposure call for the most original of Bentham's talents. For these fallacies, however beguiling, were largely of the nature of false statements of fact. Many of them are indeed pseudo-truisms and their exposure consisted very largely in rubbing people's noses in the earth of plain fact and plain language about plain fact. Why speak of learning from the wisdom of our ancestors rather than their folly? 'It is from the folly not the wisdom of our ancestors that we have so much to learn.'[2] After all, the best informed class of our wise ancestors were grossly ignorant on many subjects compared with the lowest literate class of the people in modern times.[3] How many of the laity in the House of Lords in the time of Henry the Eighth could even read? 'But even supposing them all in the fullest possession of that useful art, political science being the science in question, what instruction on the subject could they meet with at that time of day?'[4] So Bentham urges what are called old times—the wisdom of old times—ought to be called 'young' or 'early' times; for to give the name old to earlier and less-experienced generations is not less foolish than to give the name of old man to an infant in its cradle.[5] So in the very

---

[1] It was published as a paperback in 1962 (Harper Torch-books, New York).
[2] THE BOOK OF FALLACIES 401 (Bowring ed., Vol. II).
[3] op. cit., p. 400.                    [4] ibid.                    [5] op. cit., pp. 398-9.

name 'old times', says Bentham, 'there is virtually involved a false and deceptious proposition'.[1] As the last point shows, Bentham passes easily from a criticism of fact to a critique of language, and *The Book of Fallacies* has much to say under the headings of 'question-begging appellatives',[2] 'passion-kindling appellatives',[3] and 'impostor terms'[4] concerning the use, in political and moral argument, of what is now called emotive language and persuasive definition.

But behind these sources of deception Bentham saw others more insidious and less easy to identify which arose quite naturally from the very forms of human communication and reasoning. Language was, he thought, an ambiguous instrument in the sense that though possession of it raised men above the beasts (for not only communication but thought itself depended on it), yet its complex forms contained possibilities of both confusion and deception which had been exploited consciously or unconsciously by reactionary and revolutionary alike. Bentham's writings on language and on logic are among the most unsatisfactory of the Bowring texts, and a recension of them by an understanding editor is certainly overdue. Yet the main lines of his doctrines are clear. In the first place he insists on the practical utility of these studies and says they are subordinate branches of the study of Human Happiness.[5] Logic had not come to an end with Aristotle and the scholastics are blamed by Bentham both for conceiving of the subject in too narrow[6] a way and for failing to make clear what was the utility which they claimed for it.[7] In insisting on its utility, Bentham was not making an automatic gesture to his own principles. He really did think that the possibility of sane judgment in politics, and indeed in the conduct of life, depended on an awareness of the snares latent in the very texture of human discourse, the clarification of which was the province of logic.

I do not mean that his logical writings are only of value as so many blows against reaction and revolution. Besides the theory of logical constructions or 'fictions' there are many things of great speculative importance. Among these I should count his insistence on the pregnant truth 'that nothing less than the import of an entire proposition is sufficient for the giving full expression to any

[1] op. cit., p. 398.    [2] op. cit., p. 436.    [3] op. cit., p. 438.
[4] ibid.    [5] ESSAY ON LOGIC 221–2, 240–1 (Bowring, Vol. VIII).
[6] op. cit., pp. 220–32.    [7] op. cit., pp. 232–4.

the most simple thought'[1] with its important corollary that the meanings of single words are the result of 'abstraction and analysis' from sentential or propositional forms. This idea—that sentences not words are the unit of meaning—was not to appear again in philosophy for fifty years. It was then asserted by Frege[2] and stressed in Wittgenstein's *Tractatus Logico-Philosophicus*.[3] Bentham's main innovations as a philosopher are based on this insight; for he believed that the relation of language and so of thought to the world is radically misunderstood if we conceive of sentences as compounded out of words which simply name or stand for elements of reality and thus as having meaning independently of sentential forms. Philosophy—and not only philosophy—has been perennially beset by the false idea that whenever a word has a meaning there must be some existent thing related to it in some simple uniform way appropriate to the simple uniform atoms of language. Unfortunately Bentham makes this seminal point in the context of a characteristically sketchy genetic theory. He rightly contrasts his own doctrine with the Aristotelian doctrine of terms and ridicules the idea which he thinks is implicit in it: the idea that at some stage in the history of mankind 'some ingenious persons, finding these terms endowed each of them somehow or other with a signification of its own, at a subsequent time took them in hand and formed them into propositions'.[4]

How much of the course of later philosophy would have been altered had Bentham been interested enough in his own doctrine to expound it carefully and at length, or even if his few observations had been read by philosophers no one can say. Certainly no modern philosopher familiar with the metaphysical and logical perplexities which from Plato to Lord Russell were generated by the assumption that words have references or meaning apart from sentential forms, would fail to recognize the importance of Bentham's denial that this is so. But the fate of these philosophical discoveries (for such they were) of Bentham's, was the same as the fate of his best thoughts on economic analysis and policy which anticipated modern views of the power of the State to raise the level of employment and investment. In both cases, ideas now

[1] ESSAY ON LANGUAGE 322 (Bowring, Vol. VIII).
[2] *Nur im Zusammenhange eines Satzes bedeuten die Wörter etwas* DIE GRUND-LAGEN DER ARITHMETIK 73 (Breslau, 1884).
[3] London, 1933. Propositions 3.3 and 3.3:4.
[4] Bowring, Vol. VIII, p. 322.

accepted as true and important lay ignored for a century. Some of them were buried unpublished in the cellars of University College; others were published but scarcely less effectively entombed in the print of the Bowring edition.

Sometimes Bentham writes about logic in his very wide sense with an eye very closely on political argument and on the strategy for educating men into a proper awareness of its snares and pitfalls. Thus he believed that, in general, tyranny and oppression in politics were possible only where claims to infallibility of judgment were presumptuously made and stupidly conceded. It was necessary to oppose to these arrogant claims the truth that all human judgment, 'opinion', or 'persuasion' is fallible. This truth, says Bentham, 'whether for the exclusion of obstinate error, or for the exclusion of arrogance, overbearingness, obstinacy and violence [to which he added in a later passage 'bigotry'[1]] ought never to be out of mind'.[2] John Stuart Mill rightly identified this as a very important element in Bentham's teaching, and his own vindication of freedom of thought and opinion in his essay *On Liberty* is an elaboration of this same theme; for his central argument is that just because individual human judgments are fallible, freedom of thought and discussion are indispensable. But Mill does not attempt to explain why the claim to infallibility, so often made in defence of authority or the *status quo*, is false. Bentham did attempt to do this but I think failed. He thought that the falsity of all such claims to infallibility was a consequence of some simple truths about the character of human judgments; but here I think his limitations as a philosopher begin to appear. For his doctrine is the surely false one that 'of no matter of fact external to, of no matter other than that which passes in a man's own mind can any immediate communication by made by language'. He adds (using a dangerously ambiguous phrase) 'That to which expression is given, that of which communication is made is always the man's opinion nor anything more'.[3] So, according to Bentham, most of our ordinary statements of fact are elliptical and even the simplest is complex in a way not suspected by Aristotle. If, to take Bentham's example, I say that Eurybiades struck Themistocles, all I really assert and all I can assert is: 'It is my opinion that Eurybiades struck Themistocles. This is what I can be sure of and it is all that,

---

[1] op. cit., p. 321 n.    [2] op. cit., p. 300 n,
[3] op. cit., p. 321,

in relation to the supposed matter of fact, it is in my power to be assured of'.[1]

This way of disposing of claims to infallibility must be mistaken. No doubt there is an intimate and important connection between the statement (call it $p$) made by a speaker (call him $X$) on a given occasion, and the statement that $X$ believed $p$. The natural way of expressing this connection is that *in* saying $p$, $X$ *implied* that he believed it. Of course the sense of a *person* implying something by stating something needs to be clarified and distinguished from the logical relation between two statements where one entails the other. That is, we must distinguish what is implied by *what* a man says from what is implied by *his saying* it. This is perhaps not easy to do; though it is a distinction as important in the law of evidence as it is in philosophy and logic. The analysis of this relationship shows it to be of a general kind in which Bentham himself in his writings on logic and language was much interested. For it seems clear that the intimate connection between $X$ saying $p$ and his believing it, and the strangeness of saying '$p$ but I do not believe $p$', depend on the fact that one of the purposes for which human beings make statements is to invite or induce others to believe them by showing that the speaker believes them too. It may even be true that human discourse could not function as it does unless there is a generally, though not universally, respected convention that we do not say what we do not believe. But none of this supports the theory that the simplest statement is logically complex, so that in asserting $p$ we are asserting that we believe $p$. Well-known paradoxes follow from such a theory.[2] So I fear Bentham's demonstration of the fallibility of human judgments fails. Some independent analysis is required of what it is to form and hold a belief or, as Bentham calls it, an 'opinion' or 'a persuasion about matters of fact'.

I have considered this unsuccessful doctrine of Bentham's not particularly to show his limitations, but rather to show that what looks like a Philistine insistence that all studies, logic and metaphysics included, must be shown to contribute to human happi-

---

[1] Bowring, Vol. VIII, p. 321.

[2] It would follow that two speakers would not be contradicting each other if one of them said 'This is red' and the other 'No; it is not'; they would simply be comparing autobiographical notes about their beliefs. Also if the theory were correct the truth of the statement 'I do not believe this is red' would entail 'this is not red'.

ness, was in fact no such thing. For the practical ends to be served were conceived by him in no small-minded way. It was no less than that of making men conscious of the seeds of deception and confusion buried in the very texture of human thought, and so to arm them against those who would use deception and confusion to cheat them of their happiness.

## IV

So much for the intellectual armament of one set of adversaries. When Bentham turned from the logical and linguistic defences of blind custom and oppressive authority to his other adversaries— the forces of revolution and anarchy—he thought their principal appeal lay in their exploitation of the idea of an individual right. Here was the centre of the fallacies of Anarchy which tempted men to insurrection and violence by playing upon the very terminology of the law. To dispel the dangerous confusions which, as he thought, had grown or been woven round the idea of an individual's rights, he drew heavily on his doctrine of logical fictions, but his views are not merely an application of that doctrine but also of a less-explicit restrictive doctrine concerning the notion of a *reason* for an action or for feeling. His complete views on the idea of rights, legal and moral, have to be collected from a number of different texts; as widely different in subject-matter and date as the *Essays on Anarchical Fallacies,*[1] the *General View of A Complete Code of Laws,*[2] the *Pannomial Fragments,*[3] *The Limits of Jurisprudence Defined,*[4] *The Essay on Supply without Burden,*[5] and the writings on Ontology[6] and Logic.[7]

It seems to me that Bentham really was afraid not merely of intemperate invocations of the doctrine of Natural Rights in opposition to established laws, but sensed that the idea of rights would always excite a peculiarly strong suspicion that the doctrine of utility was not an adequate expression of men's moral ideas and political ideals. There is, I think, something strident or even feverish in Bentham's treatment of rights which betrays this nervousness.

---

[1] Bowring, Vol. II, pp. 500–5.   [2] ibid., Vol. III. pp. 158–60, 181–6.
[3] op. cit., pp. 217–21.   [4] (Everett ed.), pp. 55, 85, 316–18.
[5] Jeremy Bentham, I ECONOMIC WRITINGS 332–7 (ed. Stark).
[6] Bowring, Vol. VIII, p. 206.   [7] op. cit., pp. 245–8.

Bentham used his doctrine of logical fictions to dissipate the idea that words like 'duty', 'obligation', and 'right' were names of mysterious entities awaiting men's discovery and incorporation in man-made laws or social rules. Because names of logical fictions had been confused with names of real entities and had been thought to have the same simple relation with reality 'they have raised', says Bentham, 'those thick vapours which have intercepted the light. Their origin has been unknown; they have been lost in abstractions. These words have been the foundation of reasoning as if they had been external entities which did not derive their birth from the law but which on the contrary had given birth to it.'[1]

Words like 'duty', 'obligation', 'right' did indeed, according to Bentham, require the special methods of analysis which he invented for logical fictions as a substitute for the straightforward form of definition by genus and species which he held inapplicable to them. Yet, though complex in this way, statements about men's rights or duties were reducible by proper methods to statements of plain unmysterious fact. We cannot say what the words 'obligation' or 'right' name or stand for because, says Bentham, they name nothing; but we can say what statements employing these words mean. 'Obligation', indeed, was Bentham's pet example of a logical fiction and he often uses[2] as a paradigm of his methods his demonstration that to say that a man has an obligation, legal or moral, is to say that he is likely, in the event of his doing or failing to do an action, to incur the 'sanction' of official punishment or popular disapproval.

My immediate concern here, however, is with the idea of a right which Bentham considered to be 'a kind of secondary fictitious entity resulting out of a duty'[3] and in the analysis of it he certainly made some strides. The notion of an individual's right to do something or to be treated in a certain way as distinct from the notion of the right thing to do has proved most elusive even in jurisprudence where only legal rights are at stake. Part of the difficulty is that the idea is not univocal either in law or morals. There are several distinct, though not unrelated, applications of the idea of a right and theorists have often become obsessed with

---

[1] Bowring, Vol. III, p. 160.
[2] e.g., ibid., Vol. III, p. 180 and Vol. VIII, pp. 247–8.
[3] THE LIMITS OF JURISPRUDENCE DEFINED 316.

one of them to the exclusion of the others. Hobbes, for example, is almost wholly preoccupied with the important sense in which to ascribe a right to a person is to say no more than that he is neither bound to do or not to do a specific action, or (as Bentham puts it) a sense in which a right 'exists from the absence of obligation'.[1] But of course we do not mean merely this when we say that a person has a right to be paid £10 under a contract or a right to exclude others from his garden. These are cases where the right springs, as Bentham says, not from the absence of a duty but from the presence of a duty upon someone else. Here, Bentham says, what we mean in saying that a person has a right is that he stands to benefit by the performance of a duty,[2] so that all duties necessarily have correlative rights except those 'barren' duties or 'ascetic' obligations which come into existence when, as only too often, the lawmaker flouts the requirements of utility altogether and creates duties which benefit no one.[3] So much for legal rights. As for natural rights or any rights except legal rights these are not logical fictions. To talk of them is nonsense. To assert their existence is like talking of 'a species of cold heat, a sort of dry moisture, a kind of resplendent darkness'.[4] Most often men speak of such rights when bent on having their way without giving a reason for it. Such talk is 'the effusion of a hard heart operating on a cloudy mind'.[5] At its most respectable the assertion that a natural or non-legal right exists is a confusing and usually confused way of asserting that there are good reasons why men should have certain legal rights.[6] Even this is respectable only where the good reasons are those of Utility. Most often the proffered reason is Natural Law and then all is confusion; for, argues Bentham, a reason for a right is not a right (any more than hunger is food) and Natural Law is not a law.[7]

Bentham's analysis of legal rights and the accompanying *reductio ad absurdum* of the idea of non-legal rights seems to me to be mistaken. But his mistakes are illuminating. They were inherited by Mill who struggled against them with only partial success, and I do not think that the later part of Mill's *Utilitarianism* where he has much to say about both rights and duties is compre-

[1] Bowring, Vol. III, p. 181.   [2] op. cit., p. 220.
[3] op. cit., pp. 181 and 221 ff.
[4] Jeremy Bentham, 1 ECONOMIC WRITINGS 335 (ed. Stark).   [5] ibid.
[6] ibid., and Bowring, Vol. II, p. 501.
[7] Bowring, Vol. II, p. 501; Vol. III, p. 221.

hensible until we understand the difficulties to which Bentham's analysis gives rise. These difficulties spring indeed from certain fundamental features of Bentham's thought, which lie beneath the surface in many different parts of his works. They need to be brought to the surface and carefully examined. Here I can only indicate in outline the form which I think criticism should take.

Bentham's first error seems to me to be his assertion that in ascribing a legal right to an individual we are simply saying that he is a person who is likely to benefit by the performance of a correlative legal duty incumbent on another person. This view would have as its consequence that all laws, including criminal laws, which imposed duties that were capable of benefiting anyone would confer correlative rights.[1] It would follow that laws requiring military service or payment of income tax would confer legal rights on those who stood to benefit; and similarly a contract between two persons for the benefit of a third party would confer legal rights on him even if he could not himself enforce the contract. In fact, neither lawyers nor laymen treat rules of law which impose beneficial duties as always conferring rights. When they do think and speak of laws as conferring rights it is because as well as imposing duties such laws also provide, in a distinctively distributive way, for the individual who has the right. He is not merely one of an aggregate or class who are likely to benefit from the performance of some legal duty; for the idea of a right, even a legal right, is an essentially *distributive* one. According to the strict usage of most modern English jurists following Austin[2] only the rules of civil law such as torts, trusts, or contracts confer rights. Here the person who has a right is something more than a possible beneficiary of duty; he is the person who may, at his option, demand the execution of the duty or waive it. He has, in effect, a limited sovereignty over the person who has the duty and it is neither necessary

---

[1] Bentham expressly says that this is the case. 'All those words *rights obligations services offences* which necessarily enter into the civil laws are equally to be found in the penal laws. But from considering the same objects in two points of view they have come to be spoken of by two different sets of terms. *Obligations rights services* such are the terms employed in the civil code; *injunction, prohibition, offence*—such are the terms of the penal code.' Bowring, Vol. III, p. 160.

[2] LECTURES ON JURISPRUDENCE, Lecture XVII, 5th ed., p. 400. For Austin *all* the duties of the criminal law were 'absolute duties', i.e. had no correlative rights. For Bentham the only absolute duties were those the performance of which could benefit no one.

nor sufficient (though it is usually true) that he will also benefit from the performance of it.

It is, however, also true that a somewhat wider usage of the expression 'a right' is common among non-lawyers and especially among writers on political theory who might not hesitate to say, for example, that when the *criminal* law forbids murder and assault it thereby secures to individuals a right to security of the person, even though he is in no position to waive a duty imposed by the criminal law. But even in this wider usage the person said to have the right is not viewed merely as a member of a class who as a class may be indiscriminately benefited by the performance of a duty. The duty not to kill or wound or assault is unlike a duty of military service; for breach of the former duty necessarily involves the infliction of harm upon a specific or (in Bentham's language) 'assignable' individual, whereas breach of the latter duty does not but at the most merely makes it likely that the community as a whole will be less secure.[1] Thus even this extension beyond the stricter legal meaning of the idea of a right, to include *some* cases where the relevant rule and duty is one of *criminal* law, preserves still some element of the distributive character of the idea.

Thus this analysis even of a legal right fails because it neglects the peculiar provision for individuals considered distributively made by laws which confer rights. But Bentham's *reductio ad absurdum* of non-legal rights also fails because it too neglects, though in a different way, the essentially distributive character of the idea of a right. While disapproving of all talk of non-legal rights he allows, as I have said, that it sometimes has a meaning, viz., when it is simply an obscure way of asserting that there are good utilitarian reasons for creating a legal right with its corresponding duty. But here it is important to stress that though we may often insist that certain legal rights should be created simply because we believe society in the aggregate will on the whole be better off if this is done, this is not what is meant by the assertion that someone has a moral right.

A simple example may serve to show what we do mean. At the end of the last war it was decided, because of the needs of the

[1] Bentham distinguishes between offences against assignable individuals and against an 'unassignable' class or 'indefinite multitude' of individuals. But he nowhere restricts correlative rights to the former class. See PRINCIPLES OF MORALS AND LEGISLATION, Ch. XVI, §§. 2–10; Bowring, Vol. I, pp. 97–8.

economy, to give coal-miners the right of an early release from
the forces. This was widely approved, but no one who thought
they should be given this right of early release on this ground of
general utility expressed his approval by saying that the coal-
miners on these grounds had a moral right to early release. For
that statement would imply that there was a quite different sort
of reason for giving them this right; such as that the miners had
served longer than others, or more arduously, or had special
needs. I do not wish to say these references to deserts and needs
*exhaust* the class of reasons which are logically appropriate
supports for the ascription of moral rights, but they illustrate the
general character which such reasons must have. They must
refer to the present properties or past actions of the individuals
who are said to have moral rights as in themselves sufficient grounds
for treating them in a certain way independently of the beneficial
consequences to society of doing so.

It is perhaps plain from this example why Bentham could
not, without serious modification of his fundamental principles,
accommodate this aspect of non-legal rights and would have felt
bound to dismiss it as nonsense. For it involves treating something
as a reason for action which could not, according to Bentham,
*ever* be a reason. It involves looking upon something such as the
individual's deserts or past services as a reason in itself for now
doing something for him rather than for someone else. Thus to
invoke the past as in itself a determinant of the present distribu-
tion of social benefits (or burdens) was, in Bentham's eyes, mere
*ipse dixitism*—a form of intellectual bad faith which uses the
language of reason to express personal 'antipathy or sympathy',
mere irrational sentiment.

It is the principle of antipathy which leads us to speak of offences as
*deserving* punishment. It is the corresponding principle of sympathy
which leads us to speak of certain actions as *meriting* reward. This word
*merit* can only lead to passion and error. It is *effects* good or bad which
we ought alone to consider.[1]

---

[1] THEORY OF LEGISLATION 76 (trans. Hildreth, 2nd ed., London, 1867). This
quotation is wrongly referred to Bowring, Vol. I, pp. 383, 391, by Halévy in
THE GROWTH OF PHILOSOPHICAL RADICALISM, p. 55. According to C. K. Ogden
the chapter ('False methods of Reasoning on the subject of Legislation') from
which this quotation is taken is not to be found in the Bowring edition, though
the original manuscripts of it are preserved in the University College Collection
(Nos. 29 and 32). See THE THEORY OF LEGISLATION 38 (ed. C. K. Ogden, London,
1931).

This restriction on what can count as a reason dictates the character of much that Bentham has to say on responsibility, on reward, and on moral and legal obligation as well as on rights. It may also account for omissions of which Mill complained such as that of conscience from the Tables of the Springs of Action: for conscience essentially involves accepting past wrongdoing as in itself a reason for remorse and making reparation. It is indeed plain that if we were to accept Bentham's doctrine we should have to discard many concepts besides that of moral or non-legal rights; and we may interpret Bentham not as analysing but as inviting us to discard all such concepts and to substitute others more consistent with the idea of reason implicit in his general philosophy. In either case I think we have here a subject which, for two different reasons, is of considerable contemporary importance. First, the philosophical criticism of Bentham would gain in freshness and precision if it shifted from the now traditional questions to consider the extent to which his philosophy can accommodate these concepts which constitute so much of the framework of any morality. Secondly, there are many contemporary voices calling for a revision on Benthamite lines (though not exclusively for Benthamite reasons) of these concepts. Among these instances of Benthamism revived are some modern attempts to dissolve the problem of free will and to eliminate or dispense with the idea of responsibility (in some at least of the senses of that Protean word) in the treatment of offenders against the criminal law.[1]

Here I can only briefly indicate the impact of Bentham's thought on these important concepts. It is clearest perhaps in his account of the mental conditions of responsibility. According to conventional thought a very fundamental principle of justice is embodied in the doctrine that a man who has done what, so far as outward conduct is concerned, the law forbids, should not be liable to punishment or blame, if at the time of his act he was insane, a young child, or did not know that he was doing what the law forbids, or was under duress, or could not control his bodily movements. This is the doctrine, accepted in all civilized legal systems, that makes what English lawyers call *mens rea* a necessary condition of liability for serious crime. Bentham accepts this

[1] See BARBARA WOOTTON, SOCIAL SCIENCE AND SOCIAL PATHOLOGY, Chs. VIII and XI (London, 1959); and *Diminished Responsibility* 76 LAW QUARTERLY REVIEW 224 (1960).

doctrine but consistently with his general principles turns its face to the future away from the past. We are to observe such restrictions on the use of punishment not because there is any intrinsic objection to punishing a man who at the time of the crime lacked 'a vicious will' or lacked the 'free use of his will' but because his punishment will be 'inefficacious'. But Bentham does not show why such punishment *must* be useless.[1]

Bentham's analysis of obligation legal and moral similarly looks to the future away from the past, and it is this feature which, I think, renders it defective as an analysis of our actual moral and legal discourse of obligations. Stripped of its interesting complications, due to Bentham's employment of the methods of analysis which he held necessary for logical fictions ('archetypation', 'phraseoplerosis', and 'paraphrasis'),[2] the essentials of his doctrine is that to say that a man is under an obligation to do some action is to say that in the event of failure to do it he is likely to suffer: in the legal case at the hands of officials and, in the moral case, from the manifestations of general 'ill will' by the community or by his associates.[3] So, in this analysis a central place is assigned to the probability or predictability of 'sanctions', i.e. future suffering in the event of non-compliance. There is no doubt an important general connection between the probability of sanctions or of social pressure and obligation; yet the connection is not so close that the statement that someone is under an obligation is a mere assessment of the chance of suffering in the event of disobedience; for the relation between past disobedience and later suffering is not a mere *de facto* relationship of usual concomitance. This is shown by the fact that whereas in any particular case the statement that someone has an obligation to do some action may be easily combined with the assertion that he is in fact (for any of a variety of reasons) unlikely to suffer for neglecting it, it cannot be combined with the statement that his neglect of it is no *reason* why he should suffer. This is so because there is analytically involved in statements, even of legal obligation, acceptance of the idea that past action or failure to act is a reason or justification in terms of legal rules for the infliction of 'sanctions'. Where the sanctions are

---

[1] PRINCIPLES OF MORALS AND LEGISLATION, Ch. XV, pp. 84–5 and 844 (Bowring, Vol. I). See for criticism of this argument my *Prolegomenon to the Principles of Punishment* 60 PROCEEDINGS OF THE ARISTOTELIAN SOCIETY p. 4 (1959).

[2] ESSAY ON LOGIC 246–8 (Bowring, Vol. VIII).

[3] op. cit., p. 247.

predictable, this is a derivative consequence of the fact that the connection between disobedience and sanctions is looked upon in this non-predictive justificatory way.

Among the concepts which adhesion to this aspect of Bentham's thought would force us to discard or at least revise is gratitude. Here Bentham who thought and wrote much about the connected idea of reward made his position particularly clear. According to our present concept of gratitude, if we are correctly said to feel gratitude and show gratitude for past benefits it must be the case that we acknowledge past services as a reason in themselves for present feeling or action towards our benefactor. We should no longer be said to be or to feel grateful or to be applying our present concept of gratitude if our reason for returning the past service was that we should thereby encourage our benefactor or others to repeat or extend their beneficence. Saying 'Thank you' is not just a device for getting more—even for others. Bentham in thinking out when there should be *legal* rights to remuneration for past voluntary services insists that the services alone could never be reason for a reward. Only if the pactice of reward is likely to lead to beneficial consequences could there be any reason for reward. 'Reward for past services is an instrument for creating future services.'[1] As a theory of the principles on which the law should compel payment for past services this is no doubt all very good sense; but as a deduction from a philosophical doctrine concerning the idea of a reason for acting it raises disputable issues of vast importance.

What is to be said for and against accepting the restrictive concept of reason, implicit and sometimes explicit, in these parts of Bentham's work? It seems impossible to claim that this is the actual concept of reason which we already have. Yet, at certain points in his attacks on the abuse of sympathy and antipathy or *ipse dixitism*, Bentham attempts to show that it is. His arguments are chiefly developed in connection with the case of contracts or agreement where he condemns those who have failed to see that a past promise is 'no reason in itself', or in itself no 'justifying base' for an obligation. If a promise or agreement constituted a reason in itself it would always be binding but, says Bentham, it is universally agreed that certain contracts of 'pernicious tendency' should not be binding and all legal systems treat them as void.

[1] PRINCIPLES OF CIVIL CODE 340 (Bowring, Vol. I).

D

It is therefore the useful tendency of the agreement that renders it valid.[1] This argument seems to me fallacious, or at least inconclusive, though again the legal policy derived from it is very good sense. At the most such argument shows that Utility is a paramount reason which in certain cases of conflict may override other reasons. The argument shows these other reasons to be subordinate to Utility but does not show that they are derived from it.

John Stuart Mill followed very closely Bentham's analyses of obligations and rights and in Chapters III and V of his Utilitarianism sought to avoid some of the consequences. He added the 'internal sanction' of conscience to Bentham's list of the sanctions which are 'constitutive' of obligations, and he sought to make the analysis of a moral or non-legal right acceptable by insisting on the 'extraordinarily important and impressive kind of utility' on which the assertion of such rights may rest. I may be wrong in thinking that these expedients do not avoid the difficulties inherent in Bentham's restrictive doctrine of reason, but until the ramifications of this doctrine throughout both the work of Bentham and Mill have been fully considered and discussed I do not think we shall have an adequate critique of the Utilitarian philosophy.

These then are some of the topics which I think should be added to the exposition and critical discussion of Bentham. I have no doubt that an economist or political theorist could make at least as good a selection as I have made as a philosopher and a lawyer. But there are some tasks which cannot be adequately performed by one man without the co-operation of others. I hope I have made abundantly clear my conviction that of such necessarily co-operative tasks lecturing on the unread Bentham is one.

[1] PRINCIPLES OF CIVIL CODE 341 (Bowring, Vol. I). cf. RATIONALE OF REWARD, Ch. VI, p. 203 (Bowring, Vol. II).

# Dean Pound's Jurisprudence

## HERBERT MORRIS*

Justice Holmes, no mean scholar himself, referring to Dean Pound wrote, 'The number of things that chap knows drives me silly.'[1] Dean Pound's appetite for knowledge has not abated over the years. Still laboring at the age of 90, like some lone and aged giant, he has presented us with a unique and awe-inspiring work. Its three thousand pages of text are the product of practical legal experience, seventy years of study and fifty-four years of teaching jurisprudence. Commenced in 1911, it contains much material that has already been published, especially in the *Harvard Law Review* between the years 1911 and 1937. But this is no loose packaging of haphazardly connected essays, with no further justification than serving the reader's convenience. To the contrary, these essays written over the years have always had a significance beyond themselves, assuming a role in a larger endeavor—a thorough, systematic, intelligent study of law from a jurisprudential point of view.

The reader will find in these volumes what he has long associated with Dean Pound. There are historical treatments of problems which invariably supplement analytic discussion. There is his usual command of our own legal system and of foreign and ancient legal systems and materials, materials utilized always to elucidate problems of contemporary interest. There is his devoted attachment to the concrete, to the experience of men manifested in case materials, so that we continually have revealed to us the practical importance of jurisprudential issues. There is his concern for relating philosophical doctrine to the everyday legal life out of which it has arisen through reflective thought and against which

* Professor of Law and Philosophy, University of California at Los Angeles. The essay here first appeared in 13 STANFORD LAW REVIEW 185 (1960), and is reprinted here with the kind permission of the author and publisher. Copyright © 1961 by the Board of Trustees of the Leland Stanford Junior University.

[1] 2 HOLMES-POLLOCK LETTERS 115 (1941).

it must be placed to be fully appreciated. There is again and again sounded that clear and appealing note directing our attention to a legal ordering of men so that a better life for all may be realized.

Those already familiar with Dean Pound's views and jurisprudential approach will not discover, however, anything particularly novel or challenging in these volumes. Early in this century, Dean Pound seems to have fastened upon a philosophical outlook, one which demands of everything an answer to the question, 'What are you good for?', and to have devoted his energies in succeeding years more to legal scholarship, undertaken from the perspective of this functional outlook, than to continued philosophical reflection. It may be that legal philosophers, at least, will come to regard him as a horizontal rather than a vertical thinker, an accumulator of facts rather than a propounder of novel theories, one eminently sensible, remarkably erudite, but one with little passion for diving deep, one who on occasion could even urge the undesirability of doing so.[1] Those seeking an intellectual adventure, with a scope in no way bounded by concern for 'the practical', may well discover to their regret that they shall have to go elsewhere. Others may regret—as I have—the too few occasions in this work when they are pressed to object vigorously rather than assent unconcernedly, when deep philosophical differences are forced to the surface, and there is that grappling with problems which leads to an exciting step beyond conventional thought. It seems clear that Dean Pound's aim was not to make such contributions. Others may make them; he is satisfied not infrequently with classifying what they have done.

This is a work, then, of impressive proportions, but some readers will regard it as limited in serious respects. It is impossible to encompass the whole of it. I do hope however to give by a brief and selective description—sprinkled with some critical comment— the essence of what is to be found in each volume. A more detailed examination of certain topics will follow.

In the first volume Dean Pound treats the nature of jurisprudence, methods of jurisprudence, and the end of law. 'Jurisprudence' is broadly defined as 'the science of law'.[2] Developed systems of law may be examined from four jurisprudential points of view: analytical, historical, philosophical and sociological. After

---

[1] ROSCOE POUND, JURISPRUDENCE, Vol. IV, p. 530 (1959). Hereafter citations to this work are merely to volume number and page.     [2] Vol. I, p. 10.

a brief description of these methods there is a historical exposition of jurisprudential views. A lengthier consideration of nineteenth-century jurisprudential methods—analytical, historical, philosophical—follows. The common criticism of these methods is that:

they sought to construct a science of law solely in terms of and on the basis of the law itself. . . . Sociological jurists look at the methods of jurisprudence functionally. They ask, how do they work? What consequences have flowed from these methods in action? How far have they enabled the law to achieve its ends or, on the other hand, interfered with its achieving them?[1]

A major thesis of the work is that jurisprudential methods have an influence upon judicial decision and legislation. For example, analytical jurisprudence has led, in Dean Pound's opinion, to judges' operating with a jurisprudence of conceptions. This is a criticism of jurisprudential views quite apart from their correctness. Of this, more later.

He examines these methods by posing five questions:

(1) What element in the complex of phenomena that we give the name law, and what kind of system of social control through law, does it chiefly regard? . . . (2) What answer does it give to the question as to the nature of law? What is its answer to the question, how does law come into existence? (3) How does it answer the question, what makes law obligatory? What does it take to be the source of the authority of law? What does it hold gives efficacy to the legal order? (4) What form of legal precept does it take as the type? (5) What are its philosophical views?[2]

The twentieth-century schools are then considered. There are discussions of the social philosophical schools, realist schools and his own favored method, sociological jurisprudence. A full discussion of the development of sociological jurisprudence out of mechanical, biological and psychological states concludes the discussion of jurisprudential methods.

One not already well acquainted with the work of a number of men discussed in these volumes will not easily comprehend what they thought from Dean Pound's discussion. There are far too many thinkers and schools considered for thorough treatment to be given to any of them. For example, Hägerström, the leader of the Swedish realists, is given a few lines and the whole school a

---

[1] Vol. I, p. 91.    [2] Vol. I, pp. 71–4.

single paragraph.[1] These few words, it goes without saying, are
hardly helpful in learning what is going on in this important school
of jurisprudence. The work in this respect has an encyclopedic
quality. Everyone is mentioned and situated upon the jurisprudential scene, but there are few occasions where any original criticism is forthcoming.

It is regrettable, considering the encyclopedic character of his
endeavor, that Dean Pound devoted no space whatsoever to philosophical movements such as logical positivism and contemporary
linguistic analysis. One would expect in a work of this scope some
discussion of their considerable influence on thinking in jurisprudence.

To pause for a moment longer in this exposition of the work, it
should also be noted that Dean Pound's penchant for pigeonholing
and for thumbnail descriptions of philosophical positions leads him
on occasion to classifications which are certain to shock some or to
statements not easily comprehended. For an example of what I
have in mind consider this statement: 'Hart, Professor of Jurisprudence at Oxford, is with Bentham and Austin in the English
common-sense feeling of irrelevance of philosophy of law but is
tempered by the current Neo-Kantian faith in logic.'[2] Those acquainted with Professor Hart's writings may well spend a frus-
trating hour or so trying to determine the meaning of this passage.

The second part of the first volume is devoted to a historically
organized treatment of the end of law as developed in legal precepts and doctrines and the end of law as developed in juristic
thought. There is a classification of stages of legal development—
primitive law, strict law, equity and natural law, maturity of
law—and an examination of each stage's contributions and limitations. For example, in the first stage—primitive law—the end is
simply to keep the peace, and the general characteristics are: (1)
vengeance aroused and not injury suffered is the measure of dam-
ages; (2) mechanical and not rational procedures govern trials;
(3) the scope of law is limited with no principles or general ideas;
(4) the relevant unit is not so much the individual as the group.

The second volume, equally ambitious in scope, is concerned
with theories of law, the nature of law, law and morals, law and
the state, and justice according to law. The section devoted to
theories of law is brief and historical. This historical treatment is

[1] Vol. I, pp. 283-4.            [2] Vol. I, p. 80.

justified by a consideration which reveals an essential aspect of Dean Pound's thought:

much that has passed for analyses of the idea of law is little more than a generalization from the law (in the sense of the body of authoritative guides to judicial decision) of the time and place... Thus we may see how theories of the nature of the law have taken their shape and their content from the stage of legal development or the form of the body of authoritative legal materials at the time the theories were formulated.[1]

It is, for example, Dean Pound's view that English theories of the nature of law have been mostly analytical because of English parliamentary sovereignty. On the other hand, American theories in the latter part of the nineteenth century were largely historical because of our experience with judicial power and supremacy of what Dean Pound calls 'the traditional element'.

There follows a brief treatment of the practical importance of inquiring into the nature of law. As support for his view that the question 'what is law?' is a practical one Dean Pound lists several situations where courts have been required to decide upon the meaning of the word 'law'. He does not examine the question whether or not the judge's and philosopher's definitional tasks are identical and, if they are not, what differences there are between them. Nor does he consider whether or not his own definition of law, if utilized by the courts, would lead to a desirable result in each of the different cases where the word 'law' is in issue.

The discussion of the nature of law is approached according to schools. The first, considered in some detail, is the analytical school. The entire discussion takes place against the background of his own view of the nature of law which I shall discuss shortly.

Dean Pound's discussion of justice without law and justice according to law will be of special interest to those stimulated by his already well-publicized views on the administrative process. Here, once again, he is concerned with setting forth the advantages and disadvantages of different attitudes and methods. He lists, for example, six advantages of justice according to law: it becomes possible to predict the course which the administration of justice will take; it secures against errors of judgment; it secures against improper motives on the part of those who administer justice; it provides the magistrate with standards in which the ethical ideas

[1] Vol. II, p. 9.

of the community are formulated; it gives the magistrate the benefit of all the experience of his predecessors; it prevents sacrifice of ultimate interests, social and individual, to the more obvious and pressing but less weighty immediate interests.

The third volume is divided into two parts. The first treats the scope and subject matter of law and involves a consideration of Dean Pound's familiar notions of jural postulates and interests. He credits Kohler and Jhering with stimulating his thought on these concepts. In the second part he examines the sources, forms, and modes of growth of law.

Dean Pound has this comment on teaching of law and his jural postulates and interests:

> Two modes of approach have been found useful in teaching law. One is to refer the several items with respect to which legal recognition has been given or denied, and the legal precepts which have been prescribed to secure them, to jural postulates of the civilization of the time and place showing how each item corresponds to a presupposition of life in civilized society. The other is to make a classified inventory of the expectations, claims or wants asserted and calling for recognition and securing. The one mode of approach shows us what we may expect to find asserted and calling for recognition and securing, as well as the basis of recognizing and securing. The other shows what have been recognized and secured and what are pressing for recognition and securing so far as the course of legislation and adjudication can indicate.[1]

'Interests' are defined as, 'claims or wants or desires (or, I like to say, expectations) which men assert *de facto*, about which the law must do something if organized societies are to endure . . .'[2] There is little critical examination of views expressed in this part of the work. For example, while desires (and claims and wants also) seem quite different from expectations, Dean Pound casually suggests that the terms might be interchanged in his definition without affecting the sense. Is it that he regards as irrelevant any differences between claims and expectations? We can only guess that this is so and matters so essential to his jurisprudential position should not be left in doubt. Again, it is not clear to me from his discussion why law 'must do something' about interests. Does this follow from the definition of 'an interest'? Or is it rather an empirical view tacked onto the definition? If the latter, the problem arises that some interests, for example those in personality,

---

[1] Vol. III, pp. 7–8.    [2] Vol. III, p. 15.

have only recently been recognized, and in a limited way, by law. Surely, recognition of all of Dean Pound's interests is not essential to the existence of organized societies. Again, Dean Pound contributes to the controversy over whether claims are causes of law or consequences of it. It is not clear just what is being disputed here, for the words 'cause' and 'consequence' are notoriously ambiguous, but Dean Pound's view is that claims are *de facto* and that they influence legal recognition. He offers only two examples to support his view and he does not consider the possibility that there may be some claims which are consequences of law (in his sense of consequence) and some which are causes of it.[1] It seems to me that this alternative position has an initial plausibility and those interested in the dispute can only regret his failing to consider it.

As a necessary supplement to Jhering's theory of interests, he adopts an idea attributed to William James:

[A]ll the demands that press upon the legal order for recognition are to be recognized and secured so far as possible with the least sacrifice of the scheme of interests . . . as a whole. We are to try to give effect to the whole scheme with the least sacrifice of the items of that scheme. We are to order the satisfaction of claims, demands or desires with the least friction and waste. To do this requires an appraising; a weighing or valuing of the items.[2]

Little critical discussion is devoted to this proposal. The meaning of 'the least sacrifice of the scheme of interests . . . as a whole' is not obvious and very little probing should indicate how difficult it is to understand what is being proposed as an ideal. Still, this is the ideal toward which we are aiming in Dean Pound's view, and the sociological jurists attempt to aid us in reaching it through law. I will return to this question when I discuss in more detail Dean Pound's conception of jurisprudence.

There are five points which have to be considered, in his opinion, in determining the scope and subject matter of a legal system: First, we have to take an inventory of the interests which press for recognition; second, we must select and determine the interests which the law should recognize and secure; third, we must fix the

[1] Vol. III, p. 18: '[D]id working men claim a vested right in the job before or after recent legislation recognized and gave effect to it? Did the law teach workers to claim to conduct a sit-down strike or did they make the claim and their vigorously asserted claim require the legal order to do something about it?'

[2] Vol. III, p. 31. There is no discussion of 'the principles by which we determine how to appraise or weigh or value' interests in §89. See note 37 *infra*.

limits of securing the interests so selected; fourth, we must weigh the means by which the law may secure interests when recognized and delimited; finally, in order to do these things we must work out principles of valuation of interests. If I read Dean Pound correctly, while he does 'take an inventory' of interests, he provides no principles of evaluation. The traditional philosophical quest for an absolute formula is a vain one:

[H]owever common and natural it is for philosophers and jurists to seek such a method, we have come to think today that the quest is futile. Probably the jurist can do no more than recognize the problem and perceive that it is put to him as a practical one of securing the whole scheme of social interests so far as he may; of maintaining a balance or a harmony or adjustment among them compatible with recognition of all of them. Recently it has been put as a problem of integration of interests; of taking them all into account in an adjustment that gives effect to the totality so far as possible. Perhaps it would be better to say an adjustment that gives the most effect to the totality with the least sacrifice.[1]

Interests are examined from several different perspectives. There are individual, public, and social interests. Individual interests divide into interests in personality, domestic interests, and interests of substance. The latter kind of individual interest divides in turn into claims to control over corporeal things, freedom of industry and contract, claims to promised advantages, and claims to be secured against interference by outsiders with economically advantageous relations. Each of the interests is approached by way of a detailed examination of cases and statute law.

In the part dealing with sources, forms, and modes of growth are found his views on such subjects as the judicial process, legal fictions, and equity. There is a systematic treatment of the different kinds of legal problems arising for judicial determination. There is a discussion of the sources of law: usage, moral and philosophical ideas, adjudication, scientific discussion of the law, legislation. Throughout the work he is intent upon establishing a distinction between 'the traditional element' and 'the imperative element' in law. He places special stress upon the former:

[T]he traditional element is decisive as to technique and received ideals and gives and shapes doctrines and principles, conceptions and standards. The modes of growth through the traditional element are eight:

[1] Vol. III, pp. 330–1.

(1) Fictions, (2) interpretation, (3) equity, (4) natural law, (5) juristic science, (6) judicial empiricism, (7) comparative law, and (8) sociological study.[1]

There is an extensive treatment of codification, a mode of growth through the imperative element, which concludes the volume. It has much illustrative material and an examination of the theoretical disputes on codification versus noncodification.

The fourth volume is primarily devoted to an analytic inquiry into juristic conceptions. There is an extensive and interesting critique of Hohfeld. Dean Pound rejects Hohfeld's view that there is one and only one opposite and correlative for each conception. He draws principally on tort law for this discussion. While engaging in analytic inquiry, Dean Pound does not regard highly the value of such inquiry:

[T]he utility of precise terminology and exact meanings is more in connection with differentiating problems from pseudo-problems and with formulation of results than in providing solutions. None of the fundamental problems of jurisprudence is solved by terminology. There have been signs that rigid terminology has been used to create an appearance of solution of questions which have been left untouched at the core.[2]

The final volume provides a classification of the system of law. It contains, for the space taken, a remarkable survey of the law of property, contracts, torts, and criminal law. The jural postulates provide the organizing framework.

This then, in barest outline, is the monumental work of a man who has taken all of law for his province. No traditional legal problem is left unexamined. I propose to treat now in more detail Dean Pound's views on several topics. They are: the nature of jurisprudence, the nature of law, the critique of analytical jurisprudence, the analysis of 'an act'. The first three topics provide us with the core of his jurisprudential contribution, the last illustrates what I consider his chief limitation as a legal philosopher.

I

Jurisprudence is 'the science of law'.[3] As a science it consists of a 'body of critically controlled and ordered knowledge about something significant'.[4] As the science of law it has as its subject

[1] Vol. III, p. 449.  [2] Vol. I, p. 281.  [3] Vol. I, p. 10.
[4] ibid. It is not clear why the phrase 'about something significant' is added.

matter 'social control through the systematic application of the force of politically organized society',[1] or 'the legal ordering of society'.[2] It is a science, for Dean Pound, defined further in terms of certain ends other than knowledge. It seeks 'to promote and maintain an ideal relation among mankind . . .'.[3]

I have suggested thinking of jurisprudence as a science of social engineering, 'having to do with that part of the whole field which may be achieved by an ordering of human relations through the action of politically organized society'. It is an organized body of knowledge with respect to the means of satisfying human demands, securing interests, giving effect to claims and desires, with the least friction and the least waste, so far as these things can be brought about by the legal order, whereby the means of satisfaction may be made to go so far as possible.[4]

The general characteristics of the science of social engineering are: (1) its regard for the actual operation of the law rather than 'the abstract content of the authoritative precepts'; (2) its view that the authoritative guides to decision involve elements of discovery and conscious lawmaking; (3) its stress on the social purposes served by law rather than sanctions; (4) its functional attitude toward law.[5]

Dean Pound rejects the view, which he attributes to 'neo-Kantian methodologists', that there are separate sciences each with one method.[6] He also does not believe that there is one method 'all-sufficient for the science of law'.[7]

Sociological jurists . . . insist on the unity of the social sciences and the impossibility of a wholly detached, self-centered, self-sufficing science of law. They insist that the legal order is a phase of social control and that it cannot be understood unless taken in its whole setting among social phenomena.[8]

There are several difficulties raised for me by these views. I am troubled, first, by the definition of the science of law as 'an organized body of knowledge with respect to the means of satisfying human demands . . . with the least friction and . . . waste'. The characteristics of this body of knowledge and the types of legal problem upon which it will bear are not made clear. Dean Pound's language, with its mechanical overtones, may suggest to

---

[1] Vol. I, p. 16.     [2] ibid.     [3] Vol. I, p. vii.     [4] Vol. I, p. 545.
[5] Vol. I, pp. 291-3.     [6] Vol. I, p. 326.     [7] ibid.     [8] Vol. I, p. 328.

some that sociological jurists possess a kind of knowledge, or are at least working on obtaining it, which will enable us to resolve conflicts of interest in society—a problem commonly arising for legal resolution—with a minimum of friction and waste just as engineers minimize friction and waste when dealing with machines. Moral disagreements then appear as factual disagreements upon which social scientists have an authoritative say. Suppose the Supreme Court of the United States is considering the constitutionality of Bible reading in public schools. There will be a clash of interests in such a case quite similar to those which arise frequently in moral and legal disputes. Are we to read Dean Pound as suggesting that social engineers possess, or will possess, a body of knowledge which will inform judges in cases of this kind what resolution of the issue is least productive of friction and waste? If he is suggesting this, and it is taken seriously, it may lead to mistaking disagreements over values for disagreements over facts, disagreements which might be settled by further empirical inquiry. And if a precondition for intelligent disagreement is knowing what one is disagreeing about, such a suggestion may have harmful effects. As the phrase 'friction and waste' is an obscure one and as it is not enlarged upon in this work we are, in my opinion, unable to comprehend adequately the nature of the body of knowledge making up Dean Pound's science of law. We shall not know what claims can be made for it nor shall we know what type of assessment of these claims will be appropriate. Dean Pound seems so unconcerned about lines between disciplines that one is never quite sure what the characteristics of his own are. This brings me to my next difficulty.

He is critical of what he labels 'neo-Kantian methodology'. It argues for 'separate sciences' and an 'all-sufficient science of law'. He believes that having 'separate sciences' results in: 'tossing crucial difficulties about from one to the other with a result of evading them by leaving them to fall down between sharply bounded fields, in what is at bottom one science'.[1] Dean Pound's critique of these methodological views—and it should be noted that they are very sketchily treated—seems to me largely insensitive to the chief points involved. He seems to me also to have exaggerated possible harmful consequences of holding these methodological views.

[1] Vol. II, p. 284.

The neo-Kantian methodologists[1] were, first of all, intent upon maintaining a distinction between empirical and value judgments. They thought that there was such a distinction and that it was essential to be aware of it in one's work so as to avoid corrupting, perhaps unconsciously, scientific investigation. This might be done either by overlooking or failing to give proper weight to relevant factors. Weber, addressing himself to this problem, wrote:

A careful examination of historical works quickly shows that when historians begin to 'evaluate' causal analysis almost always ceases—to the prejudice of scientific results. He runs the risk, for example, of 'explaining' as the result of a 'mistake' or a 'decline' what is perhaps the consequence of ideals different from his own, and so he fails in his most important task, that is, the task of understanding.[2]

They also believed that for clear and significant arguments over evaluative matters these distinctions must be maintained. A real clash of values might be avoided by misrepresenting evaluative disputes as factual ones. Two persons might for example dispute over whether or not suicide is unnatural. They might continue their dispute, each thinking that the facts were on his side, each failing to grasp the nature of their dispute, namely, that the other is not 'blind to the facts' and that the disagreement is not resolvable in the way that factual disagreements normally are.

These methodologists were also interested in pointing out differences between 'scientific disciplines'. They thought it important to grasp the distinctions, if any, between natural and social sciences, and within the social sciences the distinctions among methods. These distinctions were emphasized so that criticism might proceed more intelligently and so that more fruitful investigation could be undertaken. They wanted us to see the world we live in—part of which is made up of a variety of modes of capturing experience—more clearly both because of the intrinsic interest of a scholar in such matters and because overlooking differences had in their opinion attendant harmful consequences. The primary point of language about 'separate sciences' is to bring to our attention these distinctions. The burden, it seems to me, is upon

---

[1] Representative of these thinkers would be Max Weber and Hans Kelsen. There is a voluminous literature on the topic. See WEBER, THE METHODOLOGY OF THE SOCIAL SCIENCES (1949); KELSEN, GENERAL THEORY OF LAW AND STATE (1945), which are essential works.

[2] WEBER, op. cit., *supra* note 27, at 33.

Dean Pound to say, first, whether or not they are valid ones. To talk about a 'unified social science', while it is an attractive-sounding phrase to rally to, does not meet the issues these methodologists have raised.

But what appears to me most objectionable in Dean Pound's exposition of these views is the impression he gives that those who have written of *'the* science of law' have in so doing ruled out inquiries that he thinks worthwhile. They merely sought to point out the differences between types of inquiries, not to argue that one rather than another of them should be undertaken. One sees this more clearly if one considers Dean Pound's views on an 'all sufficient science of law'. Kelsen has given the impression on occasion, for example, that his pure science of law was *the* science of law. He did so having in mind certain peculiarities of his approach.[1] He thought these peculiarities made it a uniquely legal science. He has never said that one interested in the relation of law to society or the evolution of law or the influence of economic factors upon legal development could employ his method to investigate such matters—indeed, the whole burden of his argument is that they cannot. And he has never adopted the view, to my knowledge, that such inquiries were unimportant. Indeed, he could agree with Dean Pound's view that law to be 'fully understood' must involve history and economics and sociology and psychology. How could he deny that if one were interested in law and economics, one must involve oneself with economics? There is nothing in 'the pure science of law' that prevents Kelsen from avowing the desirability of interdisciplinary investigation into law. He could even agree that there is no one method all sufficient for the science of law provided that the distinctions he has drawn to our attention between scientific disciplines are kept in mind. And he certainly need not take exception to a single point in the program of the sociological school.[2]

We should also bear in mind that Dean Pound holds a view not unlike that which he has attributed to 'neo-Kantians', namely that certain types of inquiry are inappropriate for the science of law. Consider this criticism of Kocourek:

---

[1] See KELSEN, op. cit., *supra* note 27, at 162–80.

[2] Vol. I, pp. 350–8. It is, consequently, not clear to me why making these distinctions will lead to 'crucial difficulties' falling 'between sharply bounded fields'.

[H]is ultra philosophical-logical analysis goes beyond what is useful in a highly practical subject. Austin rightly refused 'to thrust a treatise on intellectual philosophy into a series of discourses upon jurisprudence'. The purpose of definitions and distinctions in jurisprudence is to facilitate attainment of the ends of the legal order, not to construct a thoroughgoing metaphysic of legal conceptions and precepts.[1]

Kocourek is here read out of jurisprudence, not because his views are incorrect or inadequate, but because he has extended himself in inquiry beyond the point where the ends of the legal order are facilitated. Is it not a principal lesson of great value to be learned from the history of science that 'the practical' has much to gain ultimately from investigation not limited by concern for 'the practical'? I do not think it otherwise in jurisprudence and regret Dean Pound's suggestion that, if one continues inquiry beyond a certain point, one is no longer within the confines of 'jurisprudence'. We shall gain more, I think, from unconstrained curiosity about law than we shall from inquiry limited by our present day vision of the ends of the legal order.

## II

Let us now move on to Dean Pound's treatment of the nature of law. His approach to this subject brings to our attention elements that play an important role in the legal order. In his opinion it is a mistake in an inquiry into the nature of law to consider, as have some theorists, a single law. If we do this, we miss much that is characteristic of law. To extend our inquiry and conclude that law is 'an aggregate of rules', while an improvement, also leaves out much that is characteristic of law. It is Dean Pound's aim to draw our attention to those elements which analytical thinkers, concentrating on a rule or an aggregate of rules, have largely ignored.

He distinguishes early in the work three senses of 'law'. First, we may use the word to refer to a legal order, 'the regime of ordering human activities and adjusting human relations through the systematic application of the force of a politically organized society'.[2] Such an order, along with religion and morals, is a method of social control. When we speak of 'respect for the law' we have in mind, not just an aggregate of rules, but rather respect for a

[1] Vol. IV, p. 530.      [2] Vol. I, p. 13; Vol. II, pp. 104–5.

peculiar mode of resolving conflict in society. Second, we may refer to 'the body of authoritative grounds of, or guides to, judicial and administrative action . . . established or recognized in such a society including precepts, techniques, and received ideals'.[1] Finally, we may use the word to refer to the judicial and administrative processes.

Let us turn our attention now to 'law' in the second sense. Dean Pound is critical of analytical jurists because they have overlooked the technique and ideal elements and because they have failed to appreciate the complexity of the precept element. They have thought of precepts solely in terms of rules. Precepts, for Dean Pound, are made up not only of rules but of principles, conceptions, and standards.[2] A rule is 'a legal precept attaching a definite legal consequence to a definite detailed state of facts'. An example he gives is 'If a free man strike a free man, he shall pay ten shekels of silver'. A principle is 'an authoritative starting point for legal reasoning from which we seek rules or grounds of decision by deduction'. An example would be 'One person is not to be unjustly enriched at the expense of another'. A legal conception, such as bailment, trust, partnership, is a defined category into which cases may be fitted so that, when certain situations of fact come within the category, a series of rules and principles and standards becomes applicable. A standard, for example that of the reasonable man in tort law, is a measure of conduct prescribed by law from which one departs at his peril by answering for resulting damage or of legal invalidity of what he does.

The technique element—one example of it would be the type of reasoning by analogy that courts engage in—is

a body of traditional ideas as to how legal precepts should be interpreted and applied and causes decided, and a traditional technique of finding the grounds of decision of particular cases in the authoritative legal precepts and of developing and applying legal precepts—a technique by which the body of precepts is eked out, and the several precepts are extended, restricted, and adapted to the exigencies of the administration of justice.[3]

The ideal element involves philosophical, political, and ethical ideas as to what legal precepts should be and how the techniques should be applied. An example would be the reaction of courts in

[1] Vol. I, p. 12; Vol. II, pp. 105–6.
[2] Vol. II, pp. 124–212.    [3] Vol. I, p. 73.

E

the nineteenth century to legislation which they deemed in 'derogation of the common law'. Dean Pound nicely puts his principal point:

Each of these is an element in the everyday decision of causes. The body of precepts gets its whole life from the technique of developing and applying them; and that technique gets its color and its direction, and the precepts themselves get their shape and content for the time being, from the traditional ideas or current professional ideas as to the end of law.[1]

My own opinion is that we gain a great deal from having these distinctions brought to our attention. The picture before us now is considerably richer in its coloration and contrasts than those heretofore provided by analytical jurists who have largely disregarded the role of traditional techniques and ideals and who have concentrated almost exclusively on rules. The philosophically inclined reader will be pleased by Dean Pound's emphasis on the variety of elements which go into making up a legal order. Some may be dissatisfied, however, with his failing to go further and with his vague descriptions of the categories which he has introduced.

Among other things, it would have been desirable for him to define more precisely the type of rule he had in mind and to have noted that legal orders have rules not just of the kind he mentions, but other kinds as well.[2] To note and to elaborate upon the variety of rules becomes especially important for one interested, as is Dean Pound, in demonstrating the inadequacy of a view depicting the legal order as 'a glorified system of policing'. So distinctions here should have 'practical importance' for him. But apart from this we learn something about legal phenomena when we follow through on the question 'what is a rule?' and note that any defin-

---

[1] ibid.

[2] There are rules which require conduct: 'The right hand lane must turn right'; rules which inform us that a line of conduct is permissible: 'The right hand lane may turn right'; rules which confer powers: 'The Congress shall have the power to lay and collect taxes on income . . .'; rules which provide for immunity from having one's relations changed: 'Charitable institutions are to be exempt from liability for the torts of their employees . . .'; rules which constitute a way of doing things: 'The seats of the Senators of the first class shall be vacated at the expiration of the fourth year . . .' or 'Poker is played with fifty-two cards'; rules which define concepts: 'Treason against the United States shall consist only in levying war against them or adhering to their enemies, giving them aid and comfort'.

ing characteristics adequate for one type of rule are quite inadequate for other types. We then are led to note the differences among rules and are struck, for example, by the fact that not all rules can be violated, that some can be 'acted upon' or 'applied', but not others. When we come to wonder why these things are so and as we continue investigation, we gain a deeper appreciation of the complexity of a legal order. We learn a great deal, too, about legal orders when we consider questions like 'when does a rule "exist"?', 'what are the differences, if any, between following, acting upon, and applying a rule?', 'what are the differences between laying down, adopting, discovering a rule?' It is not by accident that these different locutions are available. They capture for us distinctions to be found in the world of legal phenomena. To be aware of them is to have a fuller grasp of the law. It is our loss that someone who has thought about the law for so long should have rested content with such a brief characterization of 'a rule'.

### III

Dean Pound's work may be viewed as, among other things, a comprehensive theoretical onslaught upon analytical jurisprudence. He is critical of its method and its substantive views. I want now to consider his functional criticism of this school. This is the crucial passage setting forth his basic criticisms:

From the sociological standpoint, the analytical method, when made the sole method in legal science, has had two serious ill consequences: (1) It led in the nineteenth century to what Jhering called a jurisprudence of conceptions, in which new situations were always to be met by deduction from traditional fixed conceptions, and criticism of the premises of legal reasoning with reference to the ends to be served was neglected. (2) The imperative theory of law—the theory of law as no more than a conscious product of the human will—has tended to lead lawmakers, both legislative and judicial, to overlook the need of squaring the rules upon the statute books or in the reports or in the doctrinal treatises, as the case may be, with the demands of reason and the exigencies of human conduct, in the case of statute law, and with the demands of social progress in the case of judge-made or jurist-made law.[1]

Before considering these criticisms, I want to examine briefly the

[1] Vol. I, pp. 91–2.

'jurisprudence of conceptions' or, as it has been labeled on other occasions, 'mechanical jurisprudence'. Once again, Dean Pound manages to devote little space to a crucial notion, one many persons immediately associate with his name, and in so doing he may leave the critical reader troubled. What are the characteristics of the jurisprudence of conceptions? Dean Pound does not make clear what they are.

An initial difficulty is that Dean Pound appears to object to judges behaving in a way that he believes it impossible for them to behave. Let us first see how this impression is given.

We learn that judges engage in a jurisprudence of conceptions when new situations are 'always to be met by deduction from traditional fixed conceptions, and criticism of the premises of legal reasoning with reference to the ends to be served [is] neglected'. Again, we find examples of it when we have 'a legal science in which conceptions are carried out logically even at the sacrifice of the ends of law, and simply for logic's sake . . . '.[1] Such language gives the impression that judges engage in mechanical jurisprudence when they allow themselves to be ruled by logic rather than by consideration of the ends of law. A conflict is set up between logic and the ends of law, and the former is victorious in mechanical jurisprudence. Consistent with this manner of thinking, there have even been those who have praised English judges for their 'distrust of logical reasoning'.[2] Mechanical jurisprudence is a slot-machine jurisprudence. Each case falls within a rule. The facts are simply put into the appropriate slot; the judge pulls the lever and the 'logically compelled' decision comes out.

That Dean Pound did not mean for us to have such a picture, although a good deal of his language on the subject supports his having meant something like it, is made relatively clear in this passage:

In such cases in the last century we could sometimes see judges following an unfortunate precedent to its more unfortunate consequences with a certain perverse relish; we could see them display a logical joy in reaching unhappy results under an assumed logical compulsion. I say 'assumed' because there was usually no logical compulsion to take the starting point that logically compelled the unfortunate result.[3]

[1] ibid.
[2] Note, 60 LAW QUARTERLY REVIEW 232 (1944); STONE, THE PROVINCE AND FUNCTION OF LAW 166 (1946).                [3] Vol. I, p. 101.

It is *not*, then, the case that judges could have met 'by deduction' new situations from traditional fixed conceptions. There must be, for Dean Pound, a decision, not logically compelled, to take as a starting point a certain principle or rule. There is only logical compulsion once the starting point is adopted. It is not 'logic', then, that is at fault but rather judges who suppose that logic compels them to do something. There are, however, difficulties with this passage.

First, why does Dean Pound say that 'there was *usually* no logical compulsion'? What types of cases does he have in mind in which there is in fact the logical compulsion to 'take the starting point'? Must we not keep steadily before us a fundamental distinction between reasoning logically and regarding oneself as bound by one's duty as a judge? It is not logic that 'binds' a judge to apply rules or to decide cases. It is his obligation as a judge to do so. He might fail in his duties as a judge without reasoning illogically. Next, Dean Pound holds that once we 'take the starting point' we are logically compelled to reach a result. But it is not clear what is involved for Dean Pound in a judge's 'taking a starting point' or in this 'logically compelling a result'.

Suppose a judge believes that a rule is clearly applicable to the facts of the case before him. Logic does not compel him to apply that rule. If he does not decide one way or the other he is an irresponsible judge, not illogical in his reasoning. If he should overrule a line of decisions, he is not illogical, though he may be, of course, unreasonable. It is not logic, but *stare decisis*, that directs him and in such cases he may be disregarding that principle but not necessarily reasoning invalidly. The judge may agree with counsel that the rule is, for example, that two witnesses are required to the signing of the will; he may agree that there was only one witness to the signing of the will in the case before him, and he still need not be 'logically compelled' to reach any result. It is always open to him to take any feature of the situation and treat it as a relevant difference. He may select any difference as relevant without being logically inconsistent. There is a difference between logical inconsistency, involving the holding of two contradictory views, and making unreasonable or absurd distinctions. This is why the expression 'carrying concepts to their logical extreme' makes little sense. As far as logic is concerned a judge can stop anywhere. But suppose that he does not overrule nor does he dis-

tinguish, what role is then played by logic in the result reached?
Judges may, indeed, set their opinions out in a form such that,
given the rule and given an additional premise, the conclusion
follows logically. But is this what Dean Pound means by 'the
starting point logically compelling a result'? The impression his
language gives is that once a judge has selected a rule, he is compelled by logic to reach a certain conclusion, and that is not so.
Logic does not compel that a valid conclusion be drawn, for logic
does not tell people to do anything. A person who agreed that 'all
men are mortal and that Socrates is a man' would not be compelled
by logic to do anything further. He can stop talking and he would
not be inconsistent. But if he draws the conclusion that Socrates is
immortal, then we may say that he is inconsistent. Neither 'starting
points' nor 'logic' compels any decision.

It is, then, still not clear from Dean Pound's presentation precisely what role is played by logic in mechanical jurisprudence. But
there are other difficulties. If we characterize mechanical jurisprudence as a judge's selecting a rule or conception and deriving implications from it without considering the effects of so doing, the
following questions may remain: First, must the judge in fact
believe that logic requires him to choose a certain rule or conception and derive certain implications? Or is it sufficient that in his
written opinion he gives the impression that logic is directing the
result? To be sure that we have an instance of mechanical jurisprudence, must we first interview a judge or have independent
knowledge of the thought processes which led him to his result?
When we charge someone with mechanical jurisprudence are we
objecting to the way he has written an opinion, setting forth his
justification for a decision, or to the way we believe he has reached
a particular result? Second, are judges who abide by *stare decisis*,
and who apply rules without considering the social effects of so
doing, guilty of mechanical jurisprudence? Third, suppose a judge
concludes that justice in a particular case requires one kind of decision and the applicable rule another. Suppose, further, that he
thinks it more important that a bad rule be applied and predictability furthered in the legal system than that a particular case be
decided on the equities. If he writes his opinion solely in conceptual terms, is he guilty of mechanical jurisprudence? Fourth, suppose the judge believes the rule a desirable one but recognizes that
in the case before him its application will not be in accord with the

equities. Suppose he decides to apply the rule but does not mention in his opinion any considerations other than conceptual ones. Is this mechanical jurisprudence? We have all had occasion to object to mechanical jurisprudence. We can pick out instances of it. What is rather more difficult to do is to pick out its essential characteristics so that we have a precise idea of what it is that we are objecting to.

Let us turn our attention now to the claim that analytical jurisprudence has had the ill consequences associated with the jurisprudence of conceptions.[1] There is nothing in Austin's jurisprudence which supports the view that judges are compelled by logic to choose particular starting points. There is nothing in analytical jurisprudence that requires a judge to follow precedent. It is regrettable that Dean Pound should make so serious an objection and not elaborate in more detail how analytical jurisprudence leads to the jurisprudence of conceptions. Here is his argument connecting analytical method with the undesirable behavior of judges:

> When we confine critical study to principles or conceptions reached by analysis and to measuring actual legal precepts by those principles and those conceptions, there is a tendency to forget that law is a practical matter. A desire for formal perfection as an end becomes controlling. Justice in concrete cases is lost sight of. Instead jurists (for practising lawyers are more in touch with reality) aim at thorough development of the logical content of established principles through rigid deduction, seeking thereby a certainty which shall permit judicial decision to be predicted in detail with absolute assurance. . . . The attempt to realize that ideal by analytical method and a jurisprudence of conceptions brings about a mechanical administration of justice which defeats its own ends.[2]

What is it that has the 'ill consequences of the jurisprudence of conceptions'? Is it analytical jurisprudence? Or is it a misconception of that jurisprudence? Or is it a misconception of one's function as a judge as Dean Pound conceives that function? Or is it an overemphasis on the importance of predictability in law? Should we simply defer in the end to Dean Pound's wealth of experience in law and suppose that work in analysis does in fact lead to 'a

[1] There are a number of different views attributed to analytical jurists. The ones here mentioned should be kept quite distinct from the method utilized by Austin or Kelsen or Hart and from a theory of law. For example, there is no essential connection between analysis as a method of jurisprudence and 'the imperative theory of law'.     [2] Vol. I, pp. 96–7.

tendency to forget that law is a practical matter'? One can only then say that it is surprising that it should be so. The analyst is then a monstrously deficient one. Analytical inquiry with Bentham and Austin and others certainly never had this consequence.

Now let us look briefly at Dean Pound's connection of analytical jurisprudence with arbitrariness:

> However true the imperative theory—that law is something made or something established consciously—however true this may be as a theory of the nature of law, it easily becomes a theory of lawmaking, and when legal science is confined to analysis of positive legal precepts and legal institutions and to an analytical and systematic critique, such a theory of lawmaking leads to bad results. Also this theory of lawmaking tends to infect judicial finding and developing of the law, with bad results. A theory of law easily becomes a theory of making law. If we are taught to exclude all ethical and social and economic elements from our science of law, and that law is the declared will of the state, or, with Gray, that it is what the courts decide because they so decide, we invite arbitrary legislation and arbitrary judicial establishing of rules.[1]

Analytical jurists have held that laws are laws whether they be good or bad laws. They have also held that while engaged in analysis, value judgments should be kept apart from analytical conclusions. The reasons for this in Bentham's case are thoroughly considered by Professor Hart.[2] There is nothing in the analytical position—I think that Dean Pound would agree with this—that precludes appraisal of laws and, indeed, in Bentham's case it was precisely his interest in intelligent formulation and appraisal which led him to insist upon analysis. We do not have any necessary connections established by Dean Pound between the imperative theory of law or the thesis of a value-free social science and arbitrary legislation and judicial establishment of rules. Rather, once again, the view is that acquaintance with the work of analysts, or doing analysis, 'tends to infect' or 'leads to bad results'.

Now I am hard put to understand why relegating value judgments to 'censorial jurisprudence', as Bentham and Austin advised, should ever lead anyone to conclude that when enacting laws they can be indifferent to whether or not they are good ones. I see nothing whatsoever in analytical jurisprudence that 'invites arbi-

[1] Vol. I, p. 98.
[2] Hart, *Positivism and the Separation of Law and Morals* 71 HARVARD LAW REVIEW 593 (1958).

trary legislation'. Any legislator or judge who supposes that analytical jurisprudence justifies an 'anything goes' attitude, or for that matter, anything that he does as a judge, is simply ignorant of analytical jurisprudence.

## IV

There is no more perplexing concept in the whole of law than that of 'an act'. Dean Pound's treatment of this topic brings out, I believe, his limitations as a legal philosopher.

Items of conduct which 'create, alter, or divest rights' or 'infringe social interests and so come within the purview of the criminal law'[1] are acts.

Acts are significant both as giving rise to or divesting rights, powers, liberties, and privileges, and creating and putting an end to duties and liabilities, and as demandable by those in whom rights, powers, liberties, and privileges inhere, and from those on whom duties and liabilities are imposed.[2]

An act is defined as 'an exertion of the will manifested externally'.[3] It is said to imply choice and is identified with a voluntary muscular motion.[4] The relevant 'external manifestation' apparently is a 'muscular motion'. Acts are then distinguished from their circumstances and from their consequences.

There is no need of saying that the circumstances surrounding the outward exertion of the will are part of the act. It is true that the circumstances under which the will is exerted may make a difference in the legal consequences. But that only shows that legal consequences of any act may be determined by something outside of itself. It is the attitude of the law toward an act which is determined by the consequences.[5]

Kocourek, in objecting to a similar definition proposed by Holmes, said ' "no one would think of saying that a contract, whether oral or written evidence of it is found, is created by a muscular contraction" '.[6] Dean Pound's response is: 'But it cannot be created without some sort of willed muscular contraction'.[7] He goes on to distinguish positive and negative acts; the latter are 'negligent omissions'.[8] The examples of acts which are provided throughout his

---

[1] Vol. IV, p. 410.  [2] Vol. IV, p. 411.  [3] Vol. IV, p. 410.  [4] ibid.
[5] Vol. IV, p. 414.  [6] Vol. IV, p. 415.  [7] ibid.  [8] Vol. IV, p. 417.

discussion are: shooting, stabbing, poisoning, beating with a club or hammer,[1] oral promises,[2] and words.[3]

Unless there has been a fundamental misunderstanding on my part, there are difficulties with every aspect of Dean Pound's treatment. They relate to: (1) the intelligibility of the definition; (2) the adequacy of the definition with respect to the purpose for which it was introduced; (3) negligent omissions as acts; (4) the compatibility of the cited examples with general definition.

Let us consider the intelligibility of the general definition. First, do we exert our will every time that we act?[4] If it is supposed that we do so, is there some experience which corresponds to this exertion? Is it a tension? Must we focus on what is going to happen? Is it anything like our exerting ourselves to lift a heavy weight? I think the difficulties suggested by such questions led Salmond to define the voluntary in terms of 'subjectible to the will', but Dean Pound does not consider this alternative.[5] Second, suppose that we agree, for purposes of discussion, that exerting our will is a recognizable experience; does this mean that whenever I do something like lifting a book or shouting, I have this recognizable experience with regard to each and every muscle that is involved in lifting the book or shouting? We shall soon retreat to a mysterious unconscious exertion of will if we adopt such a view. Third, when Dean Pound uses the words 'voluntary' and 'implies choice' are we to suppose that the voluntary and the chosen are coextensive classes? Does it follow that if an act is voluntary it is chosen? Aristotle, quite rightly, did not suppose so.[6] Fourth, when Dean Pound says that an act 'implies choice', does this mean that one must deliberate before there is an act or does it mean only that there was an available alternative? Fifth, normally, we will suppose that we only do those things voluntarily that we are aware we are doing. If Dean Pound accepts this condition, what would he say about those persons who are unaware that they are moving muscles when they do something? Are there not many people about whom we would ordinarily say they are acting voluntarily and who are quite

---

[1] Vol. IV, p. 414.      [2] Vol. IV, pp. 414–15.      [3] Vol. IV, p. 428.
[4] Dean Pound attributes to Bentham the view that 'the exertion of the will' is the 'acts'. I can find no such view anywhere in Bentham. Cited in Vol. IV, p. 413, n. 15 is BENTHAM, PRINCIPLES OF MORALS AND LEGISLATION 72 (Clarendon Press reprint 1876).
[5] SALMOND, JURISPRUDENCE 399 (11th ed., 1957).
[6] ARISTOTLE, NICOMACHEAN ETHICS, Book III.

ignorant of the muscles involved in what they are doing or for that matter of the fact that they have muscles? Are we to say about them that their muscle movements are not voluntary and hence that they have not acted?

Let us now consider the adequacy of the definition with respect to the purposes for which it was introduced. Dean Pound commenced his analysis seeking to define that item of conduct related to rights and duties, etc., in the way he had noted. For example, we know that under certain circumstances when one person crosses the property line of another or when one person fires a gun at another, certain legal consequences follow. Acts have, as is said, legal significance. But do muscular motions have this significance? Certainly not in the sense in which crossing a boundary line or firing a gun does. No rules of law treat muscular motions as a relevant legal factor, and there are obvious reasons for this. It will have been noted that Dean Pound, in responding to Kocourek, switched ground. Kocourek's objection was that the law does not regard muscular movements or contractions as legally significant. Dean Pound responded that it was at least necessary that there be such a voluntary muscular motion. But, of course, it would not follow from its being a necessary condition, supposing this were true, that the voluntary muscular motion *is* the act. At most we could infer that there would not be an act as required by law if these movements were absent.

Dean Pound's definition raises further difficulties when we reflect upon the distinction that he draws between positive and negative acts, a distinction put rather strangely: 'Again, an act may be either positive or negative, *i.e.*, acts in the narrower sense or negligent omission.'[1] Dean Pound never suggests what the 'wider sense' would be. But one would have naturally thought that if these are types of acts, the general definition of 'an act' would apply to them both. Whether or not the general definition does cover negligent omissions, and if so how, is never made clear or even discussed. We can presume that the definition does apply to omissions, for they are at one point regarded as external manifestations of the will.[2] But what is especially confusing is the limitation to '*negligent* omissions'. Why is it that intentional omissions are not included? Where are we to fit them? Most theorists have drawn a line between acts and omissions. Dean

---

[1] Vol. IV, p. 417.       [2] Vol. IV, p. 85.

Pound in his distinction suggests that there is something about the intentional omission that makes it important not to include it in his particular classification. What can it be? He does not say.

Finally, it should be apparent from the foregoing how ill-suited to his definition are the examples which are cited. It needs no pointing out that while oral promises, stabbing, shooting, and poisoning may *involve* 'voluntary muscular motions', they can hardly be identified with them. Holmes in his treatment of 'act', a treatment with which Dean Pound's has affinities, was considerably more precise, noting that the act was moving one's finger, the circumstances having a gun in one's hand, and so on.[1] By labeling 'poisoning', for example, an act, Dean Pound erases the very distinctions he thought it important to make between act, circumstances and consequences.


V


Throughout his work Dean Pound points out the 'ill consequences' of jurisprudential methods and views for law and inquiry into law. There is no mention of any such consequences associated with his own jurisprudential outlook. It is frequently very difficult to assess his views in this area and on more than one occasion I have not been convinced that he has singled out the responsible factor. Justice Holmes was apparently troubled by this feature of Dean Pound's thinking when he wrote about *Interpretations of Legal History:* 'Pound ... [has] overticketed and pigeonholed (perhaps under German influence). I don't think things so formulable ... I don't believe most judges knew or cared a sixpence for any school.'[2] Assuming, however, the general validity of Dean Pound's approach, is it far-fetched to suggest that his own views and attitudes may have certain 'ill consequences'? Does not, for example, an attitude toward analytical inquiry which both discounts its importance and places limits on how far it may go 'tend to infect' one's own analytical inquiry with the result that understanding of basic legal phenomena suffers? I think that Dean Pound's examination of 'an act' lends some plausibility to the view that it may.

[1] HOLMES, THE COMMON LAW 54 (1951).
[2] HOLMES-POLLOCK LETTERS 115 (1941).

# Kelsen and the Concept of 'Legal System'

M. P. GOLDING*

I

Among the many problems of legal theory of major importance are those which center around the concept of 'legal system'. The term 'legal system' is often used very broadly, as when we speak, for example, of the Anglo-American legal system. The late Hermann Kantorowicz, in his recently published *Definition of Law*, called any body of legal rules which had the same spatial or temporal origin a legal system. But although such broad uses are intelligible and legitimate, it is clear that legal theory requires also a more exact use of the term, a more exact concept, which will focus upon the *systematic* character of legal systems. Of course, it may be possible for a legal system to be 'systematic' in a variety of ways, and it is important to recognize that there is no privileged sense of the term 'system'. But in the last analysis legal theory will concentrate upon those senses which prove the most fruitful for the understanding and description of legal phenomena. Accordingly, we must reject any formulation of the concept of 'legal system' which would force us to distort the very phenomena which we seek to understand.

In attempting to formulate a fairly precise use (or set of uses) for the term 'legal system' and to explicate the various facets of the concept of legal system, one naturally turns to the work of Hans Kelsen.[1] It is not at all unreasonable to view this undertaking as

* Associate Professor of Philosophy, Columbia University. The essay here first appeared in 47 ARCHIV FUR RECHTS UND SOZIALPHILOSOPHIE 355 (1961) and is reprinted with the kind permission of the author and publisher.

[1] This article is based in part on a paper given at a Conference on the Present Status of Legal Positivism, held at the Villa Serbelloni, Bellagio, Italy, September 4-18, 1960. Unfortunately, Kelsen's HAUPTPROBLEME DER STAATSRECHTSLEHRE (1960) came into my hands after this paper was completed.

the master-problem of his work. Not even the most extreme anti-Kelsenite can deny that his writings illuminate this problem-area to a considerable extent, and that his influence—both positive and negative—is great.

In what follows I propose to examine the 'pure theory of law' from the viewpoint of an attempt to specify in a precise manner a sense of 'legal system' which describes accurately at least one way—perhaps the most important way—in which every legal system may be said to be genuinely systematic. My exposition turns upon an interpretation of Kelsen's theory, but I am not here concerned to argue that this interpretation represents fully the sum-total of this theory. It will be seen that this interpretation, which may be supported by a number of passages in his works, does provide an intelligible way of understanding Kelsen's position. There is no doubt that Kelsen's thought is deeply rooted in Neo-Kantianism; but the interpretation which I shall present of the 'pure theory' enables us to avoid bringing in this aspect of his philosophical background to a considerable extent.

The advantage of my interpretation is three-fold. First, it enables us to see many of the aspects in which Kelsen's theory is illuminating. Second, it enables us to see just those respects in which his theory is misleading with regard to an important kind of systematic character which legal systems do possess. In this respect, we may see that this central notion of legal system has its limitations insofar as any ongoing, complex, modern legal order is concerned. This will reveal an important feature of such systems, viz., their *open* character, as I call it. Third, by seeing just where Kelsen's theory is misleading, the lines of investigation which legal theorists and philosophers must carry out are indicated.

II

It is well known that philosophical labels are misleading, and this is true regarding Kelsen's theory of law, which is often taken as the exemplar of 'legal positivism'. Two distinctive marks have been claimed for legal positivism in general: (1) that according to it all law is man-made, and (2) that law is a social reality. These marks in particular are taken to distinguish legal positivism from natural law theories. Now whatever this claim means, it is clear that according to Kelsen at least (and also at most) one law, or legal norm, is not 'made', or 'set', or (to use his term) 'created'. I refer, of course, to the Basic Norm which is not—and indeed could not be—created, but is rather 'presupposed' or 'assumed'.[1] Regarding the second distinctive mark, Kelsen makes it quite clear, and indeed he has emphasized this probably more than any legal theorist, that law cannot be *indentified* with social facts. Although legal norms have important connections with certain social facts, which comprise their necessary conditions, legal norms cannot be reduced to any set of social facts.

Yet labelling Kelsen a legal positivist is certainly not entirely misleading. Furthermore, the term 'positivism' in this connection is suggestive and it would be of particular interest to have traced the relationships between legal positivism and the philosophical positivism of the nineteenth century, e.g., that of Auguste Comte. But here I wish to stress, in Kelsen's case, a relationship with another sort of positivism, namely, the logical positivism of the twentieth century. It would indeed be surprising if there were no relationship between the Vienna School and the Vienna Circle. In fact, it is well known that Kelsen did have personal contact with members of the Vienna Circle. There are certain obvious similarities between Kelsen's ethical theory, particularly his views on the so-called 'irrationality' of the idea of justice, and the ethical theories espoused by some logical positivists. But here I am concerned with something else.

One of the tasks which the logical positivists set for themselves is called *rational reconstruction*, although this activity is not exclusive with logical positivists and has its origins in antiquity. The logical positivists were principally interested in the natural sciences and mathematics and devoted their reconstructions to this area, while the notion of rational reconstruction is applied by Kelsen in the sphere of law or normative orders.

Briefly put, the logical positivists selected various branches of knowledge, various branches of the sciences and concepts used in the sciences, and attempted to reconstruct them on the basis of 'rational' principles. This is motivated by the following considerations. The sciences are going concerns, and scientists utilize what-

---

[1] See Kelsen's remarks on 'the limitations of positivism' in the appendix to his GENERAL THEORY OF LAW AND THE STATE 401 (1949); and cf. p. 116 [hereafter cited as GTLS].

ever concepts prove useful to the advancement of knowledge. Often a body of knowledge will develop in an unsystematic and haphazard way without a complete awareness of the assumptions employed or a clear understanding of the results attained. In a state, a branch of knowledge is ripe for 'rational reconstruction'.

An ancient example of this is the development of geometry in antiquity. It was Euclid's great achievement to reconstruct, in a 'rational' way, the results which had been attained. His reconstruction of geometry long remained the model for all rational reconstructions. Taking a relatively small set of terms as undefined, Euclid defined with precision other terms in the vocabulary of geometry. And taking a relatively small set of unproved propositions (axioms and postulates), he derived from them the hosts of theorems which had been discovered in previous centuries of research. Now what is 'rational' about Euclid's reconstruction? First, the corpus of geometrical knowledge is given a systematic order. Second, clarity is achieved through precision in definition and the reduction of the number of undefined terms. Third, it was believed that the truth of a multitude of rather complex and unevident theorems was guaranteed by deriving them from the relatively small number of axioms and postulates whose truth was held to be self-evident.

The above is the most ancient and the simplest example of a 'rational reconstruction'. Later reconstructions do not always coincide with this classical model on every point, but are related to it by a greater or lesser family-type of resemblance. Perhaps the most famous twentieth-century pre-logical positivist endeavor is exhibited in the *Principia Mathematica* of Russell and Whitehead, wherein arithmetic is reduced to logic. This work had wide ramifications, and may have contributed greatly to the development of a particular variety of rational reconstruction, namely, that of the 'ideal language'. This notion can be found in the early thought of Ludwig Wittgenstein, who influenced some logical positivists through personal contact. In his *Tractatus Logico-Philosophicus*, Wittgenstein expresses the desire to formulate an ideal language which will permit the representation of facts in their 'logical form', so that each fact is perfectly 'pictured' in the proposition which corresponds to it. For a variety of reasons, which need not be discussed here, this program was bound to fail and Wittgenstein himself ultimately rejected the position of the *Tractatus*.

The rational reconstructions of the logical positivists focused on the domain of the sciences and scientific concepts, and are less ambitious in scope than that of the early Wittgenstein. Excellent examples of such reconstructions are the respective (different) reconstructions of the concept, or concepts, of probability given by Carnap and Reichenbach. The general underlying motivation of rational reconstructions is the reformulation of a body of scientific propositions or concepts in a precise and systematic manner, employing as a base those concepts or terms which the individual reconstructionist finds philosophically acceptable. The particular philosophical significance consists in the conceptual tools employed, in terms of which the reconstruction is to be carried out, and in the justification of employing one as opposed to another base. It should also be mentioned that practical considerations play an important role in the selection and justification of the base.

The underlying motif of Kelsen's 'pure theory of law' and the relation of his legal positivism to logical positivism is the application of the notion of rational reconstruction to legal systems, or normative orders. Just as a body of knowledge of a scientific concept often needs reconstructing, so also do legal systems require rational reconstruction. This has to do with two features of legal systems—and I shall now put the matter quite broadly, and shortly indicate Kelsen's particular twist: (a) the way in which legal norms are stated, and (b) the structural relationships of legal norms within a given system. Now Kelsen does not attempt to reconstruct in detail any system of legal norms. Rather, his major contribution is theoretical, and consists in showing how the rational reconstruction of a system of legal norms is to be carried out. That is, first of all, Kelsen endeavors to provide the conceptual tools for such reconstruction, so that given any particular system of law we can construct, regardless of its content,[1] a proper representation of it. (The term 'representation', as the citations below indicate, is Kelsen's equivalent for 'rational reconstruction'.) Sec-

---

[1] In this we have the key to one of the senses in which Kelsen's theory may be said to be 'pure' or 'formal'. The general method for carrying out a rational reconstruction is applicable to every legal system, regardless of their varying content. Here we may notice a relationship with the Kantian Categories of the Understanding, which are held to be 'universal'. There are many Kantian undertones in Kelsen's thought—as in logical positivism, too!—but I cannot discuss this matter here. I should also mention that this 'neutrality' with respect to content is one of the principal points of attack against Kelsen and legal positivism by natural lawyers.

F

ondly, Kelsen undertakes to justify the use of his particular conceptual tools as opposed to those offered by some other theory of law. Naturally, it is the philosophical justification of his conceptual tools which has attracted most interest, but practical elements—some examples of which appear below—enter in as well. An interesting combination of both these sorts of justification may be found in Kelsen's criticism of legal theories which have a so-called 'ideological' bias, e.g., natural law and Marxist theories, on the grounds that if one were to follow out the implicit directions which such theories give for the reconstruction of a legal order, one would produce an incorrect or incomplete representation of the given system.

I shall now cite a few passages which indicate Kelsen's theoretical concern with the task of rational reconstruction. Kelsen distinguishes between law and the science of law, or law and jurisprudence:

It is the task of the science of law to *represent* the law of a community, i.e., the material produced by the legal authority in the law-making procedure, in the form of statements to the effect that if such and such conditions are fulfilled, then such and such a sanction shall follow. These statements, by means of which the science of law *represents* law, must not be confused with the norms created by the law-making authorities. It is preferable not to call these statements norms, but legal rules. The legal norms enacted by the law creating authorities are prescriptive; the rules of law formulated by the science of law are decriptive. It is of importance that the term 'legal rule' or 'rule of law' be employed here in a descriptive sense.[1]

Like any other empirical science, normative jurisprudence describes its particular object. But its object is norms and not patterns of actual behavior. The statements by means of which it describes norms in their specific connection within a legal order are not themselves norms. Only the law-creating authorities can issue norms. The ought-statements in which the theorist of law *represents* the norms have merely descriptive import; they, as it were, descriptively reproduce the 'ought' of the norms. It is of utmost importance to distinguish clearly between the legal norms, products of the law-creating process, which are the objects of jurisprudence, and the statements of jurisprudence. Traditional terminology shows a dangerous inclination to confuse them, and to identify law and the science of law.[2]

[1] GTLS, p. 45 (italics mine).        [2] ibid., p. 163 (italics mine).

If at all existent, the first norm (One shall not steal) is contained in the second (If one steals, he shall be punished), which is the only genuine legal norm. However the *representation* of law is greatly facilitated if we allow ourselves to assume also the existence of the first norm. . . . Law is the primary norm, which stipulates the sanction.[1]

The word in these passages to which I wish to draw attention is 'representation', which is Kelsen's term for 'rational reconstruction'. Given a legal system, the material produced by the law-making authority of a community, the function of jurisprudence, or the science of law, is to construct the 'representation' of that material.

### III

Before turning to an examination of the details of Kelsen's method of rational reconstruction, I wish to consider, in brief, two points. (I) Why have a rational reconstruction, or representation, of a legal order? (II) What is the status of such reconstructions?

(I) The answer to this question, as has already been suggested, somewhat parallels that of such questions raised regarding the reconstruction of a branch of science. Let us consider an example. Suppose we go to a locality, e.g., the State of California, and wish to know what the law of this locality is. Naturally we would avail ourselves of the written materials contained in statute books, text-books, and documents of various sorts; and also we would take account of the utterances of State executives, legislators, judges, and policemen, etc. It is clear that not every sentence encountered in these sources is a law, or legal norm. The problems which arise in identifying those sentences which are laws are considerable, but they would be relieved in great measure if there were some stand-ard way of formulating sentences which express legal norms. This supplies us with one of the first tasks of reconstruction, namely, the specification of some standard way of formulating legal norms so that they wear their legal character on their faces, so to speak. Questions arising in this connection have to do with the language of the rational reconstruction.

Kelsen believes that this task is not a mere technical problem, such that one could, for example, say that all sentences which express legal norms should be written in red ink, while non-legal

[1] ibid., p. 61 (italics mine).

sentences should be written using an ink of a different color. Such a device would be admitted to be extremely artificial by all hands. Rather, it emerges clearly from his writings that the language of the reconstruction would have to be 'ideal' in that legal norms should be expressed in it so as to exhibit their 'normative' character. For Kelsen there is a 'proper' way of formulating legal norms. I shall shortly contend that Kelsen is highly confusing in this regard, and that his position is misleading. I shall also indicate some lines of research which ought to be undertaken here.

The second sort of matter which necessitates a rational reconstruction of a legal system has to do with questions of structure. To take our example again: in examining the materials out of which we are to reconstruct the law of California, we find that not all laws, or norms, are of the same kind. Some deal with property, others with the family, others with legal procedure, and so on. And it is of course possible to systematize the materials of a legal order in the sense of classifying its parts under various headings. But while this is one possible sort of systematization, it is not the one which interests Kelsen. What concerns him is the fact that upon examining our materials we find that not all laws, or norms, are on the same 'level'. The legal norms fall into different groups, according to their positions in a scheme of *justification*. That is, some norms are justified by appealing to other norms; and the latter are, in turn, also so justified. But such appeals do not go up the steps of this hierarchy *ad infinitum*. Ultimately the chain of justifications *must* reach a final link, the *Grundnorm*, which serves the function of the *Unpositive Mover* of a system of positive law.

Viewing a legal order in this way, Kelsen points out an important fact about it. Although 'static' justificatory relations between legals norms are not excluded, relationships between norms are primarily 'dynamic' in character—or at least this is so regarding the justificatory relation of the Basic Norm to all the other norms of the particular legal order. What this means is that while it may be possible to justify a given law of a particular order, by subsuming it under another legal norm of that system, all the norms of the system cannot be justified in this manner—and, I think, Kelsen implies, it is only norms on fairly low levels of the justificatory hierarchy which are justified by subsumption. Rather, the most important sort of justification in law is to be found in an appeal to a higher norm which *delegates authority* to the agency which issues the lower norm. This crucial sort of appeal is especially applicable as regards the Basic Norm, upon which all the other laws of a legal order ultimately depend for their justification; for the Basic Norm of an order, which generally runs 'Obey the fathers of the constitution', in effect delegates authority to the formulators of the fundamental law of a given community. The justificatory relationship between the *Grundnorm* and norms falling under it is dynamic in that they 'cannot be obtained from the basic norm by any intellectual operation.'[1]

'The reason for the validity of a norm', says Kelsen, 'is always another norm, never a fact.'[2] This statement encapsulates one of the characteristic aspects of Kelsenism. A legal norm cannot be justified by appealing merely to factual 'is' statements, but only by appealing to other norms. It is the *scheme of justification* which gives us the hierarchy of legal norms, and it is this hierarchy which constitutes the *systematic* character of legal systems. Concerning this point—which is the essential contribution of Kelsen to the understanding of the concept of 'legal system'—I shall contend that Kelsen's theory is particularly one-sided, and hence inaccurate. Unless this picture of the notion of legal system is filled out in various ways, ways which still require analysis and amplification, we are bound to get a misleading picture of legal systems. We must also notice that in speaking of the justification of a legal norm Kelsen uses the term 'validity'. To justify a law *within* a given system is to establish its validity within the system. We shall also see that Kelsen obscures the subject of justification in his varied treatments of 'validity'.

(II) Having seen that the function of a rational reconstruction of a legal system is to (a) formulate legal norms in a 'proper' way, and (b) display the structure of the system, I now turn to the question of the status of such reconstructions. This question has two aspects, which happily correspond to (a) and (b).

(a) The jurisprudent—and I use this term, because 'jurist' is ambiguously used to refer both to one who studies a legal order from an external view-point and to one who operates within a

---

[1] GTLS, p. 113. E. W. Hall, in his book WHAT IS VALUE?, p. 117, remarks that this is 'a slur on the legal profession, and actually incorrect'. Unfortunately, he gives as a counter-example a legal argument which does not involve the Grundnorm. The Basic Norm may be said to be a purely formal presupposition of a legal order in that it does not by itself determine the content of the order.

[2] WHAT IS JUSTICE? 219.

legal order—who reconstructs the law of the State of California makes statements which express the law better than the delegated officials who create the law. The jurisprudent's utterances exhibit their normative and specifically legal character, according to Kelsen. But while these utterances 'descriptively reproduce the "ought" ', they are not themselves norms. This point has led to considerable trouble on the part of Kelsen's interpreters, for it suggests that according to Kelsen there is some peculiar sort of 'norm-cognition' which jurisprudents possess. Certainly there is much in Kelsen which lends itself to this interpretation, and if Kelsen has explicitly maintained this he is chargeable with obscurity. But he is not forced to maintain such a view,[1] once we remember that all he is demanding is that the reconstruction should display the normative and legal qualities of officially created law. The picture is the following: Official O, who has been delegated authority under the law of California to create law, i.e., issue authoritative legal rules, utters the statements $O_1$, $O_2$, $O_3$, $O_4$, within his legal capacity. The jurisprudent, who has no such authority, in reconstructing the law of California expresses the statements $J_1$, $J_2$, $J_3$, $J_4$, which correspond to our original set, in such a way as to bring out their normative and legal character. But the latter's utterances are not themselves legal norms, although they express the law of California. The source of the difficulty lies in Kelsen's demand that the reconstruction must exhibit the above qualities, normativity and legality. Our confusion would have been alleviated had Kelsen distinguished between *using* and *mentioning* legal utterances. The official uses the sentence

> If the situation $S_1$ obtains, then official $A_1$ ought to direct that sanctions be applied,

to govern the behavior of certain individuals. But the jurisprudent mentions the above sentence in an utterance which apprises us of the law of California. That is,

> 'If the situation $S_1$ obtains, then official $A_1$ ought to direct that sanctions be applied', is California law.

Normative jurisprudence, as Kelsen unhappily calls the jurisprudent's task of rational reconstruction, mentions laws in a particular normative and legal form; but an official can issue norms in a variety of linguistic forms.

---

[1] And in fact there are passages which may be understood as an explicit denial. See, e.g., GTLS, p. 169.

But a slight difficulty does remain. Both the official and the jurisprudent can make mistakes; they can go *wrong*. A purported legal norm of the State of California might not be issued by the appropriate authority, or might not fall within the permitted limits as to content.[1] The jurisprudent might report the law incorrectly. Kelsen maintains that the official would be wrong in the sense that his utterance is *invalid*, while the jurisprudent would be wrong in the sense that his utterance is *factually false*.[2] But our difficulty resides in the fact that we would appeal to exactly the *same* data, namely, the higher norms of the system, to show both mistakes.[3] Yet, while this is so, Kelsen seems certainly right in maintaining that there is a difference between the errors of an official of California and the errors of a jurisprudent of California. As we shall see, however, his treatment of 'validity' impedes the resolution of our slight difficulty.[4]

(b) How do the materials utilized by the jurisprudent compare with the final reconstructed legal system? Clearly, we want *all* the legal norms of California to be represented in the reconstruction. And we want the reconstruction to mention *only* legal norms. But a reconstruction is not a reproduction; there is no one-to-one correspondence between the authoritative utterances of California officials and the elements of the reconstruction. Who wants a reproduction when he can have the genuine article? The reconstruction differs from the original materials not only in the manner of formulating legal norms, but also in that the reconstruction contains more than is to be directly found in these materials.[5] This is so in that the reconstruction contains those norms which are *assumed* by officials—the most outstanding case being the Basic Norm—in order to justify the issuing of various norms. Not all the norms which legitimate the lower norms are specifically formulated by the law-

---

[1] See GTLS, pp. 134, 156. And cf. Hall, op. cit., p. 118.

[2] In this we may find another bit of support for my interpretation of the 'pure theory'. Normative jurisprudence is a descriptive science because the statements made by the jurisprudent are factually true or false. Yet Kelsen distinguishes it from sociological jurisprudence in that the latter deals with the history of a legal system, its relationship with politics, etc. The normative jurisprudent is simply concerned with reconstructing or representing the law as a system of norms.

[3] For purposes of exposition I choose to emphasize the appeal to the higher norms of the system, but, of course, factual considerations, e.g., whether a certain document was signed by a given individual, would also be relevant.

[4] See below, p. 73.          [5] Cf. GTLS, pp. 156, 161 f.

creating agencies. The jurisprudent who studies the law of California must *discover* what norms are assumed by the officials of the state. This is an important point, and I will make much of it later on. Here I wish to point out that the notion of 'legal system' is actually a presupposition of the jurisprudent. It is he who systematizes the law of California; and this he might do in a way which the officials of the state never thought or dreamt of. The key to the understanding of the concept of 'legal system' is the idea of rational reconstruction. The systematic character of a given legal order is a construction of the jurisprudent and not necessarily the fabrication of individuals who have been delegated lawmaking power.

## IV

Having expounded the purpose and method of rational reconstruction, and having intimated various criticisms, I now turn to an examination of the details of Kelsen's theory. We must keep in mind that for Kelsen the rational reconstruction of a legal order involves what I have called 'problems of language' and 'problems of structure', but before these can be approached we must first characterize the notion of 'a law', or 'legal norm'. I shall show, in this section, that Kelsen does not succeed in giving a clear-cut characterization of this notion. The idea of a legal norm is very much connected in Kelsen's mind with the topic of 'validity', therefore a good deal of what follows will turn upon this topic. It seems obvious that when we give a reconstruction of a given legal order, e.g., that of the State of California, we wish it to contain only those norms which are in some sense the valid norms of that order. But in explaining what a legal norm is Kelsen refers also to other notions, namely, rule, 'ought'-statement, binding force; and I find it difficult to correlate all he says so as to form a unitary whole. Without wishing to minimize the insights which Kelsen's analysis contains, I shall here and there suggest alternatives to it, and in particular indicate the areas which still require further investigation.

Since legal norms are, first of all, norms, let us begin with the notion of 'norm'. A norm, says Kelsen, is a 'rule forbidding or prescribing a certain behavior'.[1] Statements which express norms

[1]WHAT IS JUSTICE? 210.

are 'ought'-statements. '(T)he phenomenon of law can not be adequately described without the category of "ought".'[1] Now this is a suggestive beginning; certainly the notion of 'rule' is somehow fundamental to the analysis of law. My own feeling is that this is a good starting point for such analysis, not only because 'rule' is the more primitive notion on which the concept of law is built, but also because it is a more neutral notion. And once we see that there are various types of rules and that rules function in different ways, our analysis of law is bound to be richer and more penetrating.

But Kelsen, unfortunately, does not make his position clear. Are the three categories of norm, rule, and 'ought'-statement coextensive? Do all rules forbid or prescribe? Are all 'ought'-statements rules? Do they all forbid or prescribe? And, to bring into consideration another related topic, do all rules or 'ought'-statements impose duties or obligations? If, as I believe, they all do not do this, what are the characteristics of these rules or 'ought'-statements which do? When someone tells me that I ought to wear a coat in cold weather, is he prescribing? Is his statement a rule? What kind of rule is a law which says that a will which is not made in the presence of two witnesses is invalid? What kind of rule is this, and what, if anything, does it prescribe? Does it perhaps forbid officials from giving effect to such wills? But then must there not be other rules which indicate what ought to be done, or may be done, in such cases? What is the character of (the apparently rule-connected notion of) permissions, then?

The purpose of this barrage of questions is to point out that we have a problem-area containing a number of ideas which must be both distinguished and related. Kelsen characterizes legal norms in different ways, which lead to different results, as we shall see. He is also unclear as to where the 'ought'-element in legal norms is to be located.

According to Kelsen, legal norms are distinguished from other norms in that they are addressed to officials—strictly speaking only officials can obey or disobey the law by applying or failing to apply it in the appropriate circumstances[2]—and are sanction-stipulating. It is the 'ought'-element in them—that they prescribe that something ought to be done—which *prima facie* renders their normative character. But apparently this is not enough. In an extremely curious passage Kelsen writes:

[1] ibid., p. 215.    [2] GTLS, p. 61 f.

By 'validity' we mean the specific existence of norms. To say that a norm is valid, is to say that we assume its existence—or what amounts to the same thing—we assume that it has 'binding force' for those whose behavior it regulates. Rules of law, if valid, are norms. They are, to be more precise, norms stipulating sanctions.[1]

And again:

Validity of law means that the legal norms are binding, that men ought to behave as the legal norms prescribe, that men ought to obey and apply the legal norms.[2]

And finally:

A non-valid norm is a non-existing norm, is legally a non-entity.[3]

Here we have equated three items: existence, validity, and binding force. To say that a legal rule exists is equivalent to saying that it is valid, which is equivalent to saying that it ought to be obeyed.

The equation of the existence of legal norms and the validity of legal norms we might understand in the following way. The question 'Is $L_1$ a legal norm?' is, as it stands, nonsensical. We can not ask of any norm-like sentence whether it is a legal norm *simpliciter*. We can only ask 'Is $L_1$ a valid norm of the given legal system $S_1$?' In other words, the very notion of 'a law' or 'legal norm' requires for its analysis the notion of 'legal system'. Laws 'exist' only as elements of particular legal systems. Legal rules 'exist' only as members of systems of legal rules. To assert the existence of a legal rule is to assert the existence of a legal system to which the rule in question belongs.[4] But 'existence' in the latter case cannot mean the same as existence in the former case. Kelsen is dimly aware of this, and partly for this reason introduces the notion of the Basic Norm of a system which is—and must be—different in nature from all the other norms of the system. The recognition of the difference between these two sorts of 'existence' is marked off by the 'assumption' or 'presupposing' of the Basic Norm. Whether this is the only way of making this distinction is something which I shall not discuss here.

The above point seems clear enough, yet there are troubling things about Kelsen's triple equation. First of all, since legal norms

---

[1] ibid., p. 30.          [2] ibid., p. 39.          [3] ibid., p. 155.

[4] This point, if correct, may provide an important formal way of distinguishing between legal and moral rules. Legal rules exist only as elements of legal systems, while moral rules may be 'system-independent'. (Kelsen would, of course, deny this.)

are rules, it seems to imply that only valid norms are rules at all. But to show that an alleged legal norm is not a rule of any legal system does not, I think, deprive it of its rule-like character. (Perhaps Kelsen partially guards himself against this objection by saying that non-valid norms are *legally* non-entities.) This is particularly so if we identify a rule with an 'ought'-statement. I think that the identification of 'legal rule' and 'valid legal rule' is unfortunate as far as rational reconstruction is concerned, and below I shall suggest an alternative analysis of the 'existence' of legal rules.

The equation of the 'existence' of a legal rule with 'binding force' is even more unfortunate. This equation seems to imply that Kelsen is not satisfied to characterize a legal norm as an 'ought'-statement of a particular kind. In fact Kelsen is unsure over wherein the 'normativity' of a legal rule lies. Is it *in* the legal rule, as he sometimes suggests, or does it attach to the *whole* of the rule, or are both the case? From the above equation it would follow that what is peculiarly normative about a legal rule is not merely that it stipulates that something ought to be done, but that it (the rule) ought to be obeyed. This, I take it, is the point of identifying the 'existence' of a legal rule with its having 'binding force', that men ought to obey it.

I submit that the question whether a certain rule exists, i.e., whether a given legal rule $L_1$ belongs to some legal system $S_1$, is quite different from the question 'ought I (or anyone) obey $L_1$?' The former type of question is the province of the jurist and jurisprudent, while the latter type is the province of the moralist. It is a mistake, and a confusing one at that, to identify the 'existence' or validity of a legal rule with its having 'binding force'. Now one might, on analogy with the rules of a game, attempt the following reply to me: The identification is really not so fanciful, for to ask whether $R_1$ is a rule of chess is the same as asking whether I ought to (must) obey $R_1$, if I want to play chess.[1] However, the game-analogy, while it has its uses in legal analysis, also has its limitations. Law is not in every respect a game one can choose to play, although one can choose whether to obey or disobey the law. The anarchist who rejects the legal system of the society in which he lives can still, without contradiction, affirm a given rule to be a valid legal rule of that system.

[1] But cf. F. P. RAMSEY, THE FOUNDATIONS OF MATHEMATICS 269.

In equating the 'existence' and validity of legal rules with 'binding force', Kelsen not only treads dangerously on the ground of natural law, but also lays himself open to the charge of the natural lawyers that positivists have a concealed ideology built into their legal theory. This ideology is the most dangerous of all in its alleged complete exaltation of the State and the law-in-force. Kelsen *seems* guilty of the most severe crime of which, according to him, a legal theorist can be accused, namely, mixing theory and ideology. Does not Kelsen maintain that to say

X is a norm of legal system S in the territory T

is equivalent to saying

X ought to be obeyed by the citizens of T?

Kelsen seems to compound the crime, too, when he *seems* to give us advice on when we do not have to obey the law. After informing us that jurists consider a constitution to be valid only when the legal order based upon it is effective, he goes on to say:

The principle of effectiveness is the general basic norm that juristic thinking assumes whenever it acknowledges a set of norms as the valid constitution of a particular state. This norm may be formulated as follows: men ought to behave in conformity with a legal order only if this legal order as a whole is effective.[1]

(Notice the introduction of a new sense of 'basic norm'.) Presumably, Kelsen maintains that if a legal order is no longer effective, men do not have to behave in conformity with it.[2]

If Kelsen does maintain such a view (and I feel certain that he does not want to), then something has gone awry in the 'pure theory of law'. As mentioned above, the questions 'Is $L_1$ valid law?' and 'Ought I obey, or conform to, $L_1$?' are very different. Kelsen fails to keep his 'normative' approach to law under control; his 'normativism' is colored with moral notions. He is led into saying things which he probably does not hold. I suggest that the fault lies in his failure to grapple with the more neutral notion of 'rule'.[3]

[1] WHAT IS JUSTICE? 224.

[2] It may be that Kelsen is merely making a sociological observation about jurists. If we fit it in with the rest of his theory, I am not sure that it would take us far in the understanding of 'validity'. It would turn out that a legal order is valid on the condition that certain individuals (jurists) consider it to be valid.

[3] In one place Kelsen goes so far as to suggest that the term 'rule' be avoided in connection with law, for it invites confusion with scientific laws and also carries the connotation of 'generality'. See GTLS, p. 37 f. Here, of course, his Kantian background shows itself.

There are two more items to be noticed in Kelsen's attempt to locate the 'ought'-element, or normativity, of legal norms. First, not only is it in the consequent of the legal norm, and not only does it belong to the whole of the norm ('binding force'), but it is also in the connective joining the antecedent and consequent. 'Genuine legal norms' are hypothetical in character;[1] and so are scientific laws expressed in conditional statements. Both are 'if . . . , then—' in form. Now, according to Kelsen, in a scientific law the antecedent and consequent are causally related, and the 'if . . . , then' expresses Causation. But Causation only applies in the realm of *das Sein*, and not in the realm of *das Sollen*. Therefore, the 'if . . . , then—' in legal norms must express some other sort of relationship; antecedent and consequent must be related by a peculiarly 'normative' kind of relationship. This is the brunt of Kelsen's article 'Causation and Imputation' which is reprinted in his collection *What is Justice?* I confess that I fail to understand what Kelsen has in mind here.

A second, and more important, item about the normative or 'ought'-element in a legal norm is contained in the many places where Kelsen suggests that it derives from the higher norm which justifies the given norm. 'The reason for the validity of a norm supplies the answer to the question: why ought one behave as the norm prescribes. . . .[2] The reason for the validity of a norm is always another norm, never a fact.'[3] There is a host of problems raised by these sentences, but I shall confine myself to one remark. Kelsen distinguishes between a necessary condition (*conditio sine qua non*) for the validity of a norm, e.g., a norm-creating fact such as an act of a certain individual, and a reason for (*conditio per quam*) the validity of a norm.[4] What is meant by 'reason' here? It clearly does not mean 'sufficient condition'; but what else it could mean is never explained. Nevertheless, I think it is fairly easy to locate motivation behind this move and the item just mentioned in the previous paragraph: 'ought' and 'is' must be kept separate at all costs. Thus, the 'if . . . , then—' of legal norms must be distinguished from that of scientific laws; and the ultimate justification of a legal norm must be made to depend solely on norms. I reserve comment on this latter point until we consider 'problems of structure' in rational reconstruction.

[1] With one exception. See below, p. 88.    [2] WHAT IS JUSTICE? 218.
[3] ibid., p. 219.    [4] Cf. ibid., p. 212, and GTLS, p. 119.

Enough has been said to justify the conclusion that Kelsen fails to characterize the notion of 'a law', or 'legal norm', in a clear-cut fashion, and that it is difficult to frame what he says into a unitary whole. I shall not bother to discuss the additional complications which arise when we consider that according to Kelsen the efficacy of a legal order is a necessary (and perhaps sufficient) condition (but not the reason) for the validity of its member norms.[1]

A final word about 'existence' and 'validity', and then a suggestion or two. 'By "validity" we mean the specific existence of norms.'[2] And, according to Kelsen, the 'existence' of a norm is expressed by saying that it is 'valid'.[3] What lies behind this shift in terminology? Among other considerations, Kelsen's reasoning probably runs something like this. We say that tables exist and that norms exist, but clearly the term 'exist' does not mean the same in both instances; and it is in the later instance that the meaning of 'exist' is particularly problematic. Moreover, there is clearly a difference between making tables and issuing norms. Therefore, we ought to use another word to refer to the existence of norms, namely, 'valid'.

Now although we can appreciate the Kantian motif which in part underlies this shift in terminology, we may question its widsom. If we descend for a moment to the more primitive notion of 'rule', I can make my point rather simply. We quite naturally speak of a rule existing in a certain situation, and by this nothing mysterious may be intended. Sometimes, in saying that a rule exists, we merely mean that a rule is *applied* or *accepted*. Now I suggest that for the purposes of a rational reconstruction of a legal system 'application' and 'acceptance' are better substitutes for 'existence' than 'validity'.

Take our California example again. Suppose a California judge, wrongly believing that a certain rule is a rule of California law, applies this rule to a given case and sentences a man to suffer a given punishment. Now I do not wish to question the 'legality' or 'validity' of the judge's decision. There may very well be a rule of procedure to the effect that the result of a legal proceeding carried out in accordance with certain formal rules is a 'valid' or 'legal' result. But what about the rule which has been individualized or concretized in order to reach the decision?[4] This rule has

---

[1] GTLS, p. 41 f.  [2] ibid., p. 30.  [3] Cf. WHAT IS JUSTICE? 211.
[4] See GTLS, p. 135.

been applied in this situation, and so deserves a place in the rational reconstruction of California law—especially if the poor fellow has actually been punished as a result of the judge's decision. I am not arguing that the notion of 'validity' is useless, or that the fact that the man was punished makes this rule a valid rule of California law. In fact we might well use the notion of 'validity' in criticizing the judge's decision.[1] Rather, I maintain that in saying that a certain rule exists we sometimes simply and legitimately mean that a certain rule is, or has been, applied. This much, I think, we can learn from the American legal realists, although I do not go along with the extreme 'rule-scepticism' which some have held. Another thing they have to teach us is that it is often difficult to determine what the rules are which have in fact been applied in a given situation.[2] This goes to show that rational reconstruction is no easy matter.

Sometimes to say that a given rule exists is to say no more than that a given rule is *accepted* by various individuals. In many contexts this, too, may be a better substitute for 'existence' than is 'validity'. But it also breeds difficulties for the rational reconstruction of legal systems. Consider the case—which is not too remote from actual happenstance—of an important religious figure who is accused of committing a certain crime or violation of law, and is brought before a tribunal. While the law may appear clear cut to the judges, they may feel that it is hopeless to convict this man, because the higher court is sure to reverse them as a result of pressure brought to bear by influential persons. So instead, the tribunal exonerates him. I submit that it is no easy matter to ascertain what the rules are which are accepted in this situation. Yet 'acceptance' does seem to be a good surrogate for the 'existence' of a rule, at least sometimes.

Now it may be argued that what I have said about 'application' and 'acceptance', while relevant to other sorts of rules, does not sit well with *legal* rules and that there is need for the notion of 'validity'. But I haven't really denied the need for this notion, or some near equivalent, for use in legal criticism. Rather I am arguing that there are alternatives to Kelsen's analysis of the 'existence'

---

[1] Kelsen attempts to deal with problems of this sort in his discussion of 'Conflict Between Norms', GTLS, p. 155.

[2] See the classic article by Herman Oliphant, *A Return to Stare Decisis* 14 AMERICAN BAR ASSOCIATION JOURNAL 71–6, 107, 159–62 (1928).

of legal norms, which may do greater justice to the phenomena which legal theory seeks to understand. This point will be made with greater force in my discussion of 'problems of structure' in rational reconstruction.

V

In this section I propose to consider further some 'problems of language' in rational reconstruction. Kelsen does not regard the specification of a standard form for legal norms as a mere technical problem to be solved by merely technical devices. There is a canonical form for legal norms because 'genuine legal norms' have a specific logical character. 'General legal norms always have the form of hypothetical statements. The sanction stipulated by the norm is stipulated under certain conditions.'[1] And again: 'Having realized that the sanction is an essential element of law, he (Austin) ought to have defined the genuine rule of law as a "command" stipulating a sanction. His failure to do so involved him in contradictions.'[2]

Kelsen also rejects Austin's view that legal norms are only those which prescribe a general course of action, i.e., a class of actions which is indeterminately large. He does not do so on the grounds that Austin's criterion of generality is unworkable, but says, rather that:

The 'binding force' or 'validity' of law is intrinsically related, not to its general character, but only to its character as a norm. Since, by its nature, law is norm, there is no reason why only general norms should be considered law. If, in other respects, individual norms present the essential characteristics of law, they, too, must be recognized as law.'[3]

And in another passage Kelsen affirms that 'only the prejudices, characteristic of the jurisprudence of continental Europe, that law is, by definition, only general norms, only the erroneous identification of law with the general rules of statutory or customary law, could obscure the fact that the judicial decision continues the law-creating process from the sphere of the general and abstract into that of the individual and concrete'.[4]

It must be admitted that Kelsen is very unclear on the topic of individual norms; I shall consider them again in my discussion of the creative character of the judicial process. For our present

---

[1] GTLS, p. 38.　　　[2] ibid., p. 61 f.　　　[3] ibid., p. 38.　　　[4] ibid., p. 135.

purposes we must know that individual norms may be either hypothetical or unconditional. As examples of the latter, Kelsen refers to the sentencing of the offender, the ordering of the sanction. Thus, 'Put Jones in jail for two years!' is what Kelsen appears to have in mind as an unconditional individual legal norm.[1] I have no prejudice against such norms, but it seems to me unlikely that we wish the reconstruction of a given order to *contain* sentences which correspond to such individual norms, although we must take account of them in collecting the data for a reconstruction. Therefore, I will ignore such unconditional norms in this discussion of 'problems of language'. Because Kelsen is so vague on hypothetical individual norms, I cannot with confidence exclude them from consideration.[2]

From the above citations we see that, in rational reconstruction, (a) the canonical form of legal norms is hypothetical, and (b) the consequent of the hypothetical or conditional, is sanction-stipulating. Previously, we saw that the consequent must contain the term 'ought' or an equivalent expression. In order to facilitate the representation or reconstruction of a legal system we are permitted also to use secondary norms. These are unconditional in form, e.g., 'One shall not steal', and are not sanction-stipulating. We, Kelsen says, 'allow ourselves to assume also the existence' of secondary norms;[3] however we must realize that 'genuine legal norms' are sanction-stipulating and (with the exception which I have excluded from consideration) hypothetical.

Kelsen allows us to 'assume the existence' of secondary norms. By this he must mean that we are allowed to assume that certain secondary norms are valid norms of the particular system we are attempting to reconstruct.[4] The force of the word 'assume' is to remind us that this is a kind of fiction, which in turn depends upon

[1] ibid., p. 39; cf. p. 134.

[2] See ibid., p. 38. As an example of an hypothetical individual norm, Kelsen mentions a court decision ordering A to pay $1000 to his creditor B. This he holds to be really hypothetical in that it is equivalent to a conditional which stipulates a given sanction in the event that A does not pay the sum. I also think it unlikely that we would want a reconstruction to contain sentences which correspond to such norms. The crucial point to my mind, however, is whether Kelsen's few examples exhaust the entire gamut of the kinds of individual norm.

[3] ibid., p. 61. See also pp. 137 and 204 f. for a discussion of secondary norms from another view-point.

[4] Since Kelsen does not specifically indicate the rules whereby secondary norms are derived from primary norms, we have no way of determining which secondary norms may enter into a particular reconstruction.

G

the view that genuine legal norms are sanction-stipulating. His argument in support of this contention is a negative one. If legal norms are not sanction-stipulating, how else are we to distinguish a legal order from other kinds of normative order?[1] It is not enough, according to Kelsen, to say that legal norms are (among other requirements) norms which are 'backed up' by the threat of sanctions (as Austin would have it); each legal norm must itself be a norm which stipulates a sanction. It is in this way that the rational reconstruction of a legal order displays the character of 'legality' on its face.

I do not find Kelsen's argument convincing, and, indeed, if I accepted everything else in Kelsenism I would reject this doctrine. I do not think it necessary to draw the line between law and morals, or legal orders and moral orders, in this way. At most Kelsen's argument shows—not that all legal norms are sanction-stipulating —but that legal orders must contain (in some essential, yet to be specified manner) norms which are of this type. To show that a legal system cannot be composed exclusively of secondary norms, is not to show that it is exclusively composed of sanction-stipulating norms. But there is a more important point. There is no reason why we should not, and there is good reason why we should, regard secondary norms as genuine legal norms. Once we do this, the prejudice against nonsanction-stipulating norms is removed, and our rational reconstructions are bound to be truer to the facts.

Everyone, including Kelsen, acknowledges that law is in some sense a method of social control, and that law is in some way used by people to guide their conduct in the affairs of life. The full understanding of what this means and how this is done no doubt poses great problems. Yet we all recognize it to be so. It is in the area of control and guidance that the prescriptions or rules which Kelsen calls 'secondary-norms' have their most obvious function. And the utilization of norms of this type is not confined to the humdrum area of the life of private citizens, but is also present in the activities of official life, with all the directives and orders which govern it.

It is one of Kelsen's most important contributions to legal theory

---

[1] 'What distinguishes the legal order from all other social orders is the fact that it regulates human behavior by means of a specific technique. If we ignore this specific element of the law, if we do not conceive of the law as a specific social technique, if we define law simply as order or organization, and not as a coercive order (or organization), then we lose the possibility of differentiating law from other social phenomena . . .' GTLS, p. 26; cf. p. 122.

to have emphasized that in order for us to ascribe the character-istic of system to such a body of norms, there must also exist rules (of a different type) which enable us to *identify* such norms as ele-ments of an order. This, certainly, is the ultimate function of the *Grundnorm*. I do not question Kelsen's basic insight on this score, although I do question the details of the 'pure theory' in so far as it purports to give us a systematic account of the content, structure, and operation of legal systems in their most general aspects. And in particular, I think that the above considerations cast considerable doubt on Kelsen's conception of the 'genuine legal norm' as solely sanction-stipulating and (with our exclusion) hypothetical.

We can go even further. Kelsen grants that the Basic Norm of a legal system is not itself hypothetical and sanction-stipulating, or at least none of his examples of Basic Norms which I have seen have these qualities. In any complex legal system there may be many rules employed to identify other rules as elements of the legal system. There is no reason to imagine that these *must* be sanction-stipulating. There are many rules of procedure, governing procedure of various kinds (legislative, executive, and judicial) which can be put into the sanction-stipulating mold only on pain of distortion. There is a certain aesthetic pleasure which is derived from reducing, even distorting, all legal norms to a single canonical form. But there is no theoretical profit in it.[1] Certainly, rules which declare void certain legislative acts not carried out in accor-dance with specified procedures are rules which may be related in some intimate way to sanction-stipulating rules governing the behavior of officials relative to such acts. But there is no need to reduce the one type to the other. Consider also such a rule as

> If the price of wheat falls below that of a given index-year, then the Secretary of Agriculture shall direct that farmers be paid a given sum.

A rule of this sort is as good a candidate for a 'genuine legal norm' as any that Kelsen can imagine.

Legal rules are of different types and function in different ways. Legal theory must be sensitive to these differences and must be wary of all forms of 'reductionism'.[2]

---

[1] See, for example, Kelsen's treatment of constitutional law in GTLS, p. 143 f.

[2] It is also important to show, as Kelsen does in his treatment of the rules of substantive and adjective law, how rules of different types function cooperatively in the legal process.

## VI

I have argued, thus far, that Kelsen's views on the standard form of legal norms in the rational reconstruction of a legal order are overly restrictive and need to be supplemented in various ways. I am now going to argue that the same applies to his treatment of 'problems of structure'.

The structure of a legal order, its systematic character, derives from the fact that its norms are not all on the same 'level'. The norms find their places in a hierarchy depending on their positions in a scheme of justification. For Kelsen, to justify a norm within a given system is to demonstrate its 'validity' within that system. The notion that there is a legal justification of a norm *outside* of a legal system is nonsensical. There are no system-independent legal norms, and there is no *a priori* reason to suppose that a legal norm shown to be valid in one system can be shown to be valid in another system. Legal systems do, in fact, vary in content.

Consider our California example again. What is the method for showing that an alleged norm is a valid norm of California law? This method has two aspects, involving questions of fact and questions of law. We must first show 'the presence of norm creating fact and the absence of norm annulling fact',[1] e.g., that certain documents have been signed, etc. But this, while necessary, is certainly not sufficient, for 'the reason for the validity of a norm is always another norm, never a fact'.[2] Thus, every validation necessarily involves an appeal to a (higher) legal norm.[3] Here two things may happen, the second of which is the more basic. First, the higher norm may be a general legal norm under which the alleged norm is subsumed.[4] If this higher norm is already recognized as a norm of the system, the justification is finished. Second, the higher norm may be a norm which *delegates authority* to certain individuals to issue norms, and which declares certain acts to be law-creating facts. The first kind of justification I shall call 'justification by subsumption'; and second, 'justification by delegation'. In either case, the higher norm to which an appeal is made must itself be a valid norm of the system, and this is shown in the same ways. Ultimately we are lead up the hierarchy to the

---

[1] WHAT IS JUSTICE? 219.  [2] ibid.
[3] A set of norms may be required to demonstrate validity. For the sake of simplicity I will speak as if a single (higher) norm could always do the job.
[4] See below the discussion of the judicial process, p. 93 f.

Basic Norm of the order, whose validity we must 'assume' or 'presuppose'. The second sort of justification, i.e., by delegation, is the more basic because of the 'dynamic' character of legal systems. Somewhere along the line appeal must be made to a power delegating norm, and certainly when appeal is made to the Basic Norm. Therefore, we may think of justifications as generally being of the second type, but sometimes also involving justification by subsumption.

We may think of the process of validation as having a direction. Given any norm of a legal system (except the Basic Norm), we demonstrate its validity by appealing to a higher norm. The direction is therefore an upward one. The direction of the process of law-creation, however, is a downward one, as Kelsen pictures it. The legal system of any living society, is, thus, 'open' at the bottom. Graphically the rational reconstruction of such a legal order may be viewed as a pyramid, the bottom portions of which are continually growing. At the apex of the pyramid is the Basic Norm, and norms of lower levels are constantly being created. The 'openness' of the reconstruction is a reflection of the open and uncompleted quality of the order which has been reconstructed. So much, I believe, is implicit in Kelsen's *Stufenbau* theory, and receives an explicit expression in his conception of the creative character of the judicial process.

Although the processes of validation, or justification, and law-creation differ in direction, to Kelsen they are really the same thing viewed from different perspectives. To validate a norm (for a system) is to appeal to a higher norm of the system; to create a norm (within a system) is to apply a higher norm of the system.[1] This last point comes out in Kelsen's discussion of J. C. Gray, whose *The Nature and Sources of the Law* profoundly influenced American legal thought.[2] Against the declaratory theory of law and its mechanical conception of the judicial process Gray held that it is the judge who is the true law giver. All law is judge-made; to apply a rule of law is to create law. Kelsen, on the other hand, maintains that to create a law is to apply a law; for there is no law-creation without pre-existing law.[3] Kelsen's view is a direct consequence of his conception of 'legal norm'.

---

[1] Cf. GTLS, pp. 132 f. Of course, only state officials may create law, while both officials and jurisprudents validate.

[2] ibid., pp. 150 ff.

[3] Kelsen's discussion of Gray is not without its faults, for the term 'apply' is ambiguously employed. I cannot treat this matter here.

While Kelsen rejects the theory that *all* law is judge-made, his disagreement with Gray is not total. Both agree that judges do make, or create, law. In contrast with much of traditional legal theory this is a radical idea; legal positivism, in general, and Kelsenism, in particular, have been incorrectly assumed to necessitate a mechanical conception of the judicial process.

Wherein does the creative role of the judge consist, for Kelsen? It consists primarily (but there is another possibility which I shall shortly consider) in the individualization and concretization of general legal norms. General norms attach 'abstractly determined consequences' to 'abstractly determined conditions'. The judge employs norms of this type in arriving at decisions in particular cases. But it is *his* decision, in each case, that a particular case falls under the general norm. *He* thus determines that a given rule covers such-and-such facts, and that such-and-such facts are covered by a given rule. The judge must 'ascertain the conditioning facts'. For 'in the world of law, there is no fact "in itself" '. This function always has 'a specifically constitutive character'.[1]

In order that we may locate the 'creative' element in judicial decision, we may schematize the decision process in this way. First we have the general norm of the form.[2]

(1) If conditions C occur, then the judge shall direct sanction S against the subject X.

Then we have the hypothetical individual norm

(2) If conditions $C_1$ occur, then the judge shall direct sanction $S_1$ against $X_1$.

This norm is subsumed under (1) insofar as $C_1$, $S_1$, and $X_1$ are all concrete instances of the 'abstractly determined' C, S, and X. Next we have the judge's statement as to the 'conditioning facts'.

(3) $C_1$ has occurred.

And finally, the judge's ordering of the sanction

(4) $S_1$ against $X_1$! (e.g., 'Put Jones in jail for two years!')

Insofar as the judicial process concerns the individualization and concretization of general norms, the above seems to be the general pattern into which such decision-making fits.[3] A fuller account of

---

[1] ibid., p. 135 f.                          [2] But cf. ibid., p. 136.

[3] Kelsen's exposition often suggests that a legal system grows through the concretization and individualization of general norms. Does he then think of legislation itself as the concretization and individualization of procedural rules?

this topic would require the development of the logic of normative sentences. It must be noticed that in the area of civil law Kelsen holds sentences like (4) to be unnecessary, since he regards them as equivalent in meaning to sentences of type (2). In any case, the creative element in judicial law-making enters in by way of (3). However sentences like (3), while they are 'judicial acts' in some sense, are not legal norms. Since (2) is subsumed under (1), there is nothing particularly 'creative' in the issuing of hypothetical individual norms. The only genuinely new legal norm would be (4), which, I think, is uninteresting from a jurisprudential point of view. The above schematization is not exclusively confined to the judicial process, but obtains in all areas of the governmental process, e.g., executive agencies, where general rules are applied to particular cases.

Judicial decision-making is creative also in that courts may exercise a legislative function.[1] This is obvious in cases where judges have the power to annul pieces of formal legislation. But judges are also creative when their decisions have the character of precedent. Unfortunately, Kelsen is extremely sketchy on this matter. The 'binding force' of the general norm which is obtained by generalizing the individual norm 'is the essence of a so-called precedent'.[2] Kelsen does not treat the problems which surround the generalizing of 'norms which determine the behavior of one individual in one non-recurring situation and which therefore are valid only for one particular case and may be obeyed or applied only once'.[3] Even if we could solve these problems, there is another serious difficulty. In order to be consistent Kelsen must hold that a judicial decision has the character of a precedent in a system only if there is a rule of the system which gives it this character. What would such a rule be like? I submit that it is no easy matter to formulate such a rule, especially if it must be put into the Kelsenite canonical form. In the case of executive agencies of government there are many clear-cut examples of power-delegating rules which authorize the creation of general rules of substantive law.

The above sketch of judicial law-creation must now be considered in relation to 'problems of structure' in rational reconstruction. Whenever judges create laws, individual or general legal norms, they must justify their creations, show that the new norms

---

[1] GTLS, pp. 149 f; p. 272.      [2] ibid., p. 149.      [3] ibid., p. 38.

are valid norms of the system. Kelsen recognizes two ways of demonstrating validity, namely, justification by subsumption and justification by delegation. The structure of a system, as it is represented in the reconstruction of a Kelsenist jurisprudent, is a reflection of these two kinds of justification. The place which a particular judge-made norm has in the structure is determined by the higher norm which is 'applied' in its creation in order to justify it.

Now I wish to argue that the reconstruction of the structure of a legal system in this way, especially that of a living system of a modern society, is bound to be misleading and partial. A Kelsenite reconstruction would force us to cast the structure of such systems into unrealistic molds. A Kelsenite reconstruction presupposes that a legal system, while 'open' at the bottom, is nevertheless 'closed' at the top. It assumes that we can always recognize the norms which are, or may be, 'applied' in order to justify an instance of law-creation, and that such norms 'pre-exist' such instances. (It must be recognized that 'application' is ambiguous. To 'apply' a rule of substantive law is not the same as 'applying' a power-delegating rule.) But this is not always the case. Those rules which do 'pre-exist' may change and shift the range of their application. More importantly, judges not only decide cases, but also make rules, formulate principles, and enunciate standards in order to decide cases. Creation goes on in the upper parts of the system as well as the lower. Kelsen is dimly aware of this but does not see its significance for rational reconstruction. The rules, principles and standards which judges frame in the deciding of cases deserve to be reflected in the jurisprudential reconstruction of legal systems. The advantages of attempting a Kelsenite reconstruction may lie in its very shortcomings. It may reveal just those areas in the system which are 'open'.

The inadequacies of Kelsen's type of rational reconstruction, and another feature of 'openness', are seen when we consider whether the justifications which judges give may all be reducible to subsumption and delegation. For example, judges apply the standard of 'public interest' in a variety of decision-areas. Officials, generally, apply all sorts of standards in the granting of licenses.[1] To reduce the methods of justification in these areas to subsump-

---

[1] For Kelsen's treatment of legal norms as standards see WHAT IS JUSTICE? 209 f., 230.

tion and delegation would be an oversimplification. The pure theory of law is misleading insofar as it reduces legal justification to these two kinds. Here again is an area which demands the attention of legal theorists and philosophers.

To say that judges, or other officials, are rule-makers, are creative, is not to say that they are *ipso facto* arbitrary. We do not think of the artist as arbitrary just because he is creative. (The bad, uncreative artist does things arbitrarily.) Of course, the artistic analogy has its limitations in this context, and I do not wish to over-stress it. My essential point is that rule-makers do, in general, attempt to justify their creations in various ways, which are not confined to delegation and subsumption. A rational reconstruction of a legal system must reflect all types of justification. To limit a reconstruction of structure to the two types of justification which Kelsen considers will not give us an accurate picture of the system. And if I am correct concerning the 'open' character of the systems of complex societies, no reconstruction will be complete. A more compelling feature of 'openness' will be brought out in the next section.

VII

The last item of the Pure Theory which I shall discuss is the Basic Norm. There are many questions which this notion elicits, but my examination here deals with it only in connection with 'problems of structure' in rational reconstruction. We have already en-countered some of Kelsen's reasons for maintaining that there must be a Basic Norm at the apex of the reconstruction of a legal order. I shall argue that this matter may be more complicated than Kelsen's account suggests.

Above I presented in outline the way one would go about recon-structing the legal system of the State of California (or any other territory).[1] While the jurisprudent, following Kelsen, knows that the system has a structure with certain general features, it is obvious that he does not know what the structure is—i.e., the hierarchy of norms—in advance of an actual examination of the inchoate materials which constitute his data. This does not mean that jurisprudents always begin a reconstruction in a state of total ignorance. If one had no idea of where to look, what sources to

---

[1] *supra*, pp. 13 and 11.

take into account, no reconstruction could even get off the ground.

Now if I am correct in saying that the simplest and most natural sense of the 'existence' of legal rules is that such rules are applied, then the materials which merit special attention in reconstruction are those rules which are actually applied by officials. Second, the jurisprudent must attend to those rules and those sources to which officials appeal in justifying their actions. Out of these a rough picture of the structure begins to emerge. The picture is given precision, again following Kelsen, by fitting in to the appropriate places also those rules which are assumed by officials in order to validate their official pronouncements.[1] The picture is completed when we are able to specify the Basic Norm of the system.

Rational reconstruction can be done only in this piecemeal, step-by-step fashion. It begins at the bottom and works its way towards the top. There is no jurisprudential Geiger Counter which clicks when we approach a higher norm. The relative positions of norms within the structure can be determined only after a complicated inquiry into their respective functions. Moreover, it is no easy matter to state with precision the exact norm (or set of norms) which validates a given lower norm, for there may be, in any given case, a number of alternative putative higher norms which would do the job. These methodological difficulties become magnified when the jurisprudent must identify the norms which officials implicitly assume. Naturally, the formulations the jurisprudent settles on will depend upon what he already knows about the contents of the system. Therefore, a step-by-step approach must be blended with a broader, but tentative, view of the system.

Because reconstructions begin at the bottom of the pyramid, gradually working towards the apex, the jurisprudent does not begin the reconstruction of the law of a territory already knowing the Basic Norm which ties together all the norms and all the validations. Again, we have no machine which informs us of the Basic Norm.

If I am right, there follows an important jurisprudential consequence. *There is no a priori reason for maintaining that there is*

---

[1] The word 'assume' hides a hornets' nest of problems. Consider the differences among what is 'logically assumed', what is 'consciously assumed', and what is 'unconsciously assumed'. Kelsen is not clear on what he has in mind. See, for example, GTLS, p. 116, where Kelsen says that the Basic Norm is 'what all jurists, mostly unconsciously assume'; while on the other hand the Basic Norm 'really exists in the juristic consciousness'.

*a single, specific Basic Norm which is assumed by all the law-making officials of a territory.* To put the point graphically, there is no reason for holding that a reconstruction, and especially the system of which it is a reconstruction, have the shape of a pyramid. As we go up the levels of the hierarchy we may find that our reconstruction branches off in different directions. There may be disconnections among the higher norms. The key to this matter may very well be the meaning of 'assume' or 'presuppose'. We may discover that the law-making officials do not all 'consciously assume' or 'logically presuppose' the same higher norms. It is not such a remote possibility that—as paradoxical as it sounds—there is more than one Basic Norm operative in California law, for example.

Kelsen would not, I believe, accept this conclusion. He supposes that each legal system and each reconstruction separately constitutes a unity. There can be only one Basic Norm for each system. His argument in this connection curiously parallels medieval arguments for the existence and unity of the Godhead.[1] We may also compare his dogma that there can be no contradiction between an inferior and superior norm of a system with the doctrine of Pre-established Harmony. No contradictions arise because the jurisprudent explains them away by supposing that the norms of the system are otherwise than they really are?[2] In this way the unity of a system is preserved. Moreover, Kelsen argues, if we do not suppose that there is but one single Basic Norm how are we to identify a group of norms as belonging to the same legal order?

Kelsen's views and arguments in these regards throw into relief the extent to which his conception of 'legal system' is an *ideal* construct. In general, there may be no harm in attempting to make reality in the image of our ideals. But it is certainly at least conceptually harmful to suppose that reality already conforms to our ideals. What Kelsen has done is to formulate an ideal conception of 'legal system', to which any legal system may approximate. But if we go about reconstructing a system in the manner in which I have indicated, we may see how remote any system is from this ideal. If I am not mistaken, this throws into question the utility of Kelsen's concept of 'legal system' for legal theory. I do not now propose to show what the uses of this concept may be, but I think that I have said enough to indicate the respects in which it may

[1] See GTLS, p. 124.    [2] ibid., p. 161 f.

mislead us. We must again rethink the concept of 'legal system' and, as a corollary, the topic of 'validity'. If the jurisprudent is able to explain away contradictions between the norms of a system either by supposing that the higher norms are different from what they initially seem to be or by introducing new norms, then it would seem that he implicitly uses criteria other than the already 'existent' higher norms in order to determine what the valid norms of the system are.

## VIII

In closing this paper, I again wish to emphasize that I have treated the 'pure theory of law' from only one possible point of view, that of rational reconstruction. I do not think that this exhausts the entire significance of Kelsen's legal thought. But it does serve to sharpen Kelsen's theory so that we can see its merits and its shortcomings. If we still criticize Kelsen today, it is a testimony to the fertility of his thought. Along the way I have raised more problems than I have solutions for; but the work of the legal theorist and philosopher is far from complete.

# Professor Fuller on Morality and Law

ROBERT S. SUMMERS*

### INTRODUCTION

The *Morality of Law*[1] will find a place among the important books in the history of American legal philosophy. It includes insights into the relations between morality and law, and advances a theory of law of great practical relevance. Since 1947, its author has been Carter Professor of Jurisprudence at the Harvard Law School. Though he has written many articles and book reviews,[2] *The Morality of Law* is only his second book on legal philosophy. His first, *The Law in Quest of Itself*,[3] was published in 1940, and was widely reviewed.

During his long and distinguished career, the author of *The Morality of Law* has done his share of thinking about such 'staples' of legal philosophy as: the relations between morality and law,[4]

* Professor of Law, Cornell University. The essay reprinted here first appeared in 18 J. LEGAL EDUCATION 1 (1966) and is reprinted with the permission of the publisher.

[1] LON L. FULLER, THE MORALITY OF LAW (1964). [New Haven: Yale University Press, 1964. Pp. vii, 202. $5.00.] This volume is an expanded version of the Storrs lectures which the author delivered at Yale Law School in April 1963. Page references in the text are to this volume.

[2] Among the reviews of books on legal philosophy are the following: Ogden, *Bentham's Theory of Fictions* (1932), in 47 HARV. L. REV. 367 (1933); Pound, *Formative Era of American Law* (1938), in 34 ILL. L. REV. 372 (1939); Hall, *Readings in Jurisprudence* (1938), in 87 U. PA. L. REV. 625 (1939); Bodenheimer, *Jurisprudence* (1940), in 41 COLUM. L. REV. 965 (1941); Jones, *Historical Introduction to the Theory of Law* (1940), in 55 HARV. L. REV. 160 (1941); Adler, *Dialetic of Morals* (1941), in 9 U. CHI. L. REV. 759 (1942); Buckland, *Some Reflections on Jurisprudence* (1945), in 59 HARV. L. REV. 826 (1946); Paton, *A Text-book of Jurisprudence* (1946), in 59 HARV. L. REV. 383 (1948); Reuschlein, *Jurisprudence— Its American Prophets* (1951), in 12 LA. L. REV. 531 (1952); Hale, *Freedom Through Law: Public Control of Private Governing Power* (1952), in 54 COLUM. L. REV. 70 (1954); Patterson, *Jurisprudence: Men and Ideas of the Law* (1953), in 6 J. LEGAL ED. 457 (1954).

[3] Foundation Press, Inc.

[4] See especially, Fuller, *Positivism and Fidelity to Law—A Reply to Professor Hart*, 71 HARV. L. REV. 593 (1958), and the instant book.

the nature of law,[1] judicial reasoning,[2] legal fictions,[3] problems of interpretation,[4] and theories of punishment.[5] But he has not been content with the traditional subject-matter of legal philosophy. He has defined new problems and given new twists to old ones. Thus, he invented what he calls 'eunomics'—the study of 'natural laws of forms of social order'.[6] He has been deeply interested in the problems of modern economic planning.[7] He has fought hard against what he deems scientism in law and legal theory.[8] He has written at length on the 'relation' between fact and value, and has tried to show the folly of thinking about social ends apart from their means of implementation.[9]

This diversity of interests, and a decidedly practical bent, pervade *The Morality of Law*. But in this review-article, we shall focus only on what the author says about the nature of morality, the nature of law, and the relations between these phenomena. And we shall not dwell on the many virtues of his book. Instead, we shall criticize, and at length. The book is obviously an 'articulation of views that have been in the making for many years'.[10] It therefore deserves systematic evaluation.

One final introductory remark: Criticism always involves hazards of interpretation. If we have misread the author, perhaps we

[1] See the citations in the preceding footnote and Fuller, *American Legal Realism*, 82 PA. L. REV. 429 (1934); Fuller, *Pashukanis and Vyshinsky: A study in the Development of Marxian Legal Theory*, 47 MICH. L. REV. 1157 (1949); and Fuller, *American Legal Philosophy at Mid-Century*, 6 J. LEGAL ED. 457 (1954).

[2] Fuller, *Reason and Fiat in Case Law*, 59 HARV. L. REV. 376 (1946).

[3] Fuller, *Legal Fictions*, 25 ILL. L. REV. 363, 513, 877 (1930–31).

[4] See especially, Fuller, *Positivism and Fidelity to Law—A Reply to Professor Hart*, 71 HARV. L. REV. 630, 661–9 (1958).

[5] Fuller, *The Case of the Speluncean Explorers—In the Supreme Court of Newgarth, 4300*, 62 HARV. L. REV. 616 (1949).

[6] See Fuller, *American Legal Philosophy at Mid-Century*, 6 J. LEGAL ED. 457, 473 (1954); Fuller, *Adjudication and the Rule of Law*, 1960 PROCEEDINGS AM. SOC. INTERNAT'L. L. 1; Fuller, *Collective Bargaining and the Arbitrator*, 1963 WISC. L. REV. 3.

[7] See Fuller's extended review of Hale, *Freedom Through Law: Public Control of Private Governing Power*, in 4 COLUM. L. REV. 70 (1954); and Fuller, *Freedom— A Suggested Analysis*, 68 HARV. L. REV. 1305 (1955).

[8] This fight is carried on in many of his published writings.

[9] See especially the exchange between the author and Professor Ernest Nagel of Columbia University: Fuller, *Human Purpose and Natural Law*, 3 NATURAL L.F. 68 (1958); Nagel, *On the Fusion of Fact and Value: A Reply to Professor Fuller*, id. at 77; Fuller, *A Rejoinder to Professor Nagel*, id. at 83; Nagel, *Fact, Value, and Purpose*, 4 NATURAL L. F. 26 (1959).

[10] A phrase once used by the author in a review-article. See Fuller Book, Review 54 COLUM. L. REV. 70 (1954).

may take solace in the fact that cries of 'But you have misread me!' are endemic in legal philosophy. Of course, we do not imply that the author would disagree with all that we say in what follows. As he himself once said in a review-article: 'Since I am throughout taking issue with [the author] . . ,. it will be hard to avoid conveying the impression that I believe that . . . [he] . . . would say the opposite of everything I say. This is, of course, not the case'.[1]

## I. THE NATURE OF MORALITY

The author's first chapter, 'The Two Moralities', is a contribution to moral philosophy and should be assessed as such. In his opening paragraph, he says 'existing literature' on the relationship between morality and law is unsatisfactory since, he thinks, legal philosophers have not clarified 'the meaning of morality itself' (p. 3).[2] He then sets out to clarify it for us. His approach is to 'emphasize a distinction between . . . the morality of aspiration and the morality of duty'.[3] Three questions naturally arise: Is this a sound *approach*? How well does the author contrast and relate 'the morality of aspiration' and 'the morality of duty?' And, of what utility is his distinction between these 'two moralities?'

### A. Soundness of the Author's General Approach
The author sets out to 'clarify the meaning of morality itself'. But there is no such thing. 'Morality' has several meanings and many uses. Moreover, the author is not really interested in the meanings of words as such, but in phenomena—in the nature of morality.[4]

---

[1] Fuller, Book Review, 6 J. LEGAL ED. 457, 458 (1954).

[2] For relevant discussions by moral philosophers, see Urmson, *Saints and Heroes*, in ESSAYS IN MORAL PHILOSOPHY 198 (Melden ed., 1958); Strawson, *Social Morality and Individual Ideal*, 36 PHILOSOPHY 1 (1961); MORRIS GINSBERG, ON THE DIVERSITY OF MORALS IN 1 ESSAYS IN SOCIOLOGY AND SOCIAL PHILOSOPHY (1956). See also, Frankena, *Recent Conceptions of Morality*, in MORALITY AND THE LANGUAGE OF CONDUCT 1 (Castenada ed., 1963), where it is said: 'Contemporary moral philosophy may, therefore, be represented as primarily an attempt to understand what morality is. . . .'

[3] This distinction has recently been considered by Professor H. L. A. Hart of Oxford. See H. L. A. HART, THE CONCEPT OF LAW 176–80 (1961). For the writer's extended consideration of this book see Summers, *Professor H. L. A. Hart's Concept of Law*, 1963 DUKE L. J. 629.

[4] The writer has recently argued at length that talk of *definition* of law and *definition* of morality should be abandoned, for it only invites confusion. See Summers, Book Review, 53 CALIF. L. REV. 386 (1965).

And it is morality as contrasted and related to law that he wishes to clarify. Yet even this use of 'morality' is ambiguous. Is the author interested in morality as it is—'popular morality'? Or in morality as it ought to be? He does not always make this clear. Sometimes he appears to be writing of popular morality, or a branch of it; at other times, about morality as it ought to be.[1]

Can morality be satisfactorily explained by emphasizing a distinction between 'the morality of duty' and 'the morality of aspiration?' No wholly satisfactory answer can be given, because the author does not tell us what specific confusions or unclarities he hopes to clear up in this way. Without knowledge of these, we have no specific standards against which to judge the success of his enterprise.[2]

If we say, simply, that his purpose is just to clarify morality 'in general', then, as a first step, we may expect him to set about drawing distinctions. And he does distinguish between his two moralities.[3] Yet to draw this distinction in terms of duties and aspirations is misleading, for it suggests that the performance of moral duties is not something to which we can aspire, which is false.[4] Perhaps 'moral duties' and 'moral ideals' would be better nomenclature.[5]

But further distinctions are necessary. Moral duties break down into affirmative actions and forbearances. Indeed, in ordinary usage, 'duty' is often confined to affirmative actions.[6] For this reason, and also because of differences between acts and forbearances, some moral philosophers prefer 'moral duties' and 'moral prohibitions' to 'affirmative and negative duties'.[7] What of ideals? These break

---

[1] Compare, for example, the references to the Ten Commandments on p. 6 and the list of examples of 'negative' duties on p. 42, with the 'critical' morality he seems to espouse at the top of p. 7.

[2] Cf. Whitely, *On Defining Morality* 20 ANALYSIS 141 (1960).

[3] See Urmson, *supra* note 16, at 198–9.

[4] See text preceding note 29, *infra*.

[5] Even this way of putting it may mislead. Thus, devotion to duty as such is an ideal, and, in some circumstances, we may idealize the performance of particular duties.

[6] Thus it sounds a bit odd (except, perhaps, to lawyers) to speak of our *duty* not to steal or not to fornicate. It has been argued that duties are attached to social roles, e.g., parent, fiduciary, etc.; whereas prohibitions, e.g., do not steal, are not thus confined and apply more or less universally. See Harrison, *Moral Talking and Moral Living*, 38 PHILOSOPHY 315, 318 (1963). One important implication of this view is that people's duties vary considerably.

[7] See Urmson, *supra* note 16, at 198.

down into at least two basic subcategories: personal virtues, e.g., courage; and social ends, e.g., justice.[1] Each of these should be distinguished from 'ways of life' having moral worth. And, 'ways of life' break down into those that are 'personal', e.g., 'the life of contemplation', and those that are 'social', e.g., 'a life of dedicated service to others'. The foregoing distinctions are not inconsequential. Each marks out a significant component of morality. And still more sorting could be possible.[2]

Thus the internal complexity of morality may be clarified via distinctions of the foregoing kinds. Such distinctions pave the way for a second step, which is to ask: What are the relations between the various component 'parts' of morality? This question, in turn, gives rise to different sub-questions. For example, may duties and ideals conflict? Is there some part of morality that is in some sense the foundation of the whole? Do some parts of morality operate as a 'check' on other parts?

There is also an essential third step. The first two steps concern the internal complexities of morality. But how is morality to be contrasted with other social phenomena? Such contrasts ordinarily illuminate, and the analysis of internal complexities does not inevitably turn up differentiating features or throw them into bold relief. The author dwells only on the very general distinction between duties and ideals, a distinction within morality rather than between morality and other phenomena. He does not consider, for example, how moral and non-moral ideals are to be differentiated. Yet it is clear that there are non-moral ideals, both personal and social.

Thus, in sum, the author's *approach* to the clarification of morality cannot be adequate to the task. He does not tell us whether he is clarifying morality as it is or as it ought to be. The distinctions he undertakes to draw are sufficient only to provide the crudest account of the internal complexities of morality. And he fails to contrast morality with other social phenomena, thus depriving his analysis of whatever illumination the identification of differentiating features might provide.

---

[1] At p. 12, the author himself hints at such a distinction.
[2] A shift in point of view is essential if we are not to neglect important features of morality. See, for example, the illuminating remarks on moral consciousness in Harrison, *supra* note 24, at 324–7.

H

## B. *Contrasts and Relationships Between Moral Duties and Moral Aspirations*

What are some of the ways the author contrasts and relates his two moralities? First, he stresses that the morality of duty embodies the 'most obvious demands of social living',[1] while the morality of aspiration 'is . . . the morality of the Good Life, of excellence, of the fullest realization of human powers' (p. 5). But does the author mean that the morality of duty embodies *only* the 'obvious demands of social living'? If so, his two moralities, as he distinguishes them, do not exhaust the whole of morality. Many duties cannot be characterized as 'obvious demands of social living'. Indeed, for perhaps ninety-nine percent of all Americans, the most prominent ingredient of morality consists of duties not to engage in various sex activity. Yet observance of many of these duties is hardly vital to social life. How might the author object to this criticism? He might say, simply, that he nowhere says his morality of duty encompasses all moral duties. But if this should be his response, then we may ask, what, for him, constitutes the 'morality of duty'? Only those duties that he thinks *ought* to be considered 'obvious demands of social living'? He does not say. Nor does he make explicit the criteria he would use to determine what moral duties are essential to social life. Furthermore, insofar as the author's morality of duty turns out to be no more than his own view of what that morality ought to be, then, to the extent that it differs from prevailing morality, it can be of little value in contrasting and relating morality as it is and law as it is.

According to the author, a second contrast between the morality of duty and the morality of aspiration is that we do not praise men for doing their duties but we do praise them for moral excellence (p. 30). But it is false that we do not praise men for doing their moral duties. One who generally does his duties comes in for praise. And so do others: A, an expert swimmer, saves a drowning child from a swimming pool. B, who is chronically ill, continues to work each day to support his family. C, a young damsel, sacrifices her social life to care for her aged and widowed father. D, who has

[1] See also pp. 6, 9, 27, 30. The author uses interchangeably the following phrases: 'most obvious demands of social living', 'Basic requirements of social living', 'Conditions obviously essential to social life', 'minimum conditions of social living'. Yet each of these phrases has a distinct meaning. Also, 'social living' and 'social life' are exceedingly vague expressions.

promised something to another, performs his promise, though this is financially disastrous for him. In each of these and in many other examples that come to mind, there is something to praise, and something to aspire to. Yet in each there is performance of a duty.[1]

Third, the author suggests that the morality of duty 'normally requires only forebearances', while the morality of aspiration is in some sense affirmative (p. 42). But such duties as the duty to keep one's promises, to care for another, to support one's family, or to help someone in distress are all both affirmative and common. Furthermore, the morality of aspiration, for some persons, consists very largely of a life of abstinence.

According to the author, a fourth difference between his two moralities is that the morality of duty can be enforced (more or less) by law, whereas the morality of aspiration cannot (pp. 9, 42). But many have thought moral duties of the sort just instanced to be quite difficult to enforce by law. Furthermore, we cannot always separate the impact of law from that of other social forces in the way the author implies. To take one important illustration: public school education is compulsory in many societies. And, we may hope, many students 'compelled' to attend learn some things that incline them later to lead the good life. In some such cases, has not compulsion played a part?

Fifth, the author says moral duties are 'sticky' and inflexible while 'it is the nature of all human aspirations toward perfection... to be pliable and responsive to changing conditions' (p. 29). But how could this be established? By massive cross-cultural research? And we may doubt that it is the nature of *all* human aspirations toward perfection to be pliable. We can bring to mind many ideals *fixées* in the history of mankind.

The author describes a sixth difference between his two moralities:

. . . as we leave the morality of duty and ascend toward the highest levels of a morality of aspiration, the principle of marginal utility plays an increasing roll in our decisions. On the level of duty, anything like economic calculation is out of place. In a morality of aspiration, it is not only in place, but becomes an integral part of the moral decision itself— increasingly so as we reach toward the highest levels of achievement (p. 44).

[1] Moral ideals also influence the *way* moral duties are performed. Thus we may tell the truth in a spirit of kindness and sympathy. See ROBERT S. DOWNIE, GOVERNMENT ACTION AND MORALITY 24 (1964).

But this is not wholly true. Something quite like economic calculation does take place in those many instances in which persons resolve conflicts of moral duties. In such cases, the 'limited resource' is simply that only one course of action is possible, and the 'opportunities' the costs of which are to be measured consist of two courses of action each of which is required by some moral principle. Choice between these, when made on the basis of such 'measurement', can, without distortion, be characterized as 'something like economic calculation'.

Seventh, the author suggests that judging a man to have conformed to moral aspirations is an 'essentially subjective and intuitive process' whereas judging a man to have done his duty is not (pp. 13–14, 30–2). This phraseology suggests that the author may really have more than one difference in mind. He might mean that judgments of duty are somehow 'objective'—rationally defensible —whereas the adoption of moral aspirations is more 'subjective'— less rationally defensible. Or he might also mean that we can 'discover' our moral aspirations[1] only by some process of intuition whereas we can tell what our moral duties are in particular cases by more rational methods. The author does not sort out these two possible contrasts. And he does not *argue* for either. Yet both pose issues that have been highly controversial in moral philosophy.

The author is not clear about an eighth possible contrast between his two moralities. While the writer cannot be sure he has understood Fuller, he seems to suggest that in persuading others to do their duties, we use techniques different from the ones we use when we try to get others to recognize certain ideals (pp. 20, 14–15). What he says about the former is this:

What the Golden Rule seeks to convey is not that society is composed of a network of explicit bargains, but that it is held together by a pervasive bond of reciprocity. Traces of this conception are to be found in every morality of duty, from those heavily tinctured by an appeal to self-interest to those that rest on the lofty demands of the Categorical Imperative. Whenever an appeal to duty seeks to justify itself, it does so always in terms of something like the principle of reciprocity. So in urging a reluctant voter to the polls it is almost certain that at some point we shall ask him, 'How would you like it if everyone acted as you propose to do?' (p. 20).

---

[1] There is a further ambiguity here. The author might mean either 'discover what our moral aspirations are' or 'discover what they ought to be'.

Now the foregoing passage involves at least three very different questions which the author does not sort out. These are: (1) How can a particular duty be justified? (2) How do we in fact persuade another to do his duty? (3) How can we justify being moral at all? The first and second questions are clearly distinct, and are both quite different from the third. We can justify 'being moral' without saying anything about particular duties. And what is a good reason for being moral may be entirely without force in justifying a conclusion that some action is a duty. Thus the probability that others will reciprocate is a good reason for being moral,[1] yet this tells us little about what our specific duties should be. Which of the three foregoing questions interests the author? From his discussion, all three appear to, though he does not keep them distinct. But what he does say about how we in fact persuade others to do their duties is false, and, therefore, can reveal no contrast with how we get others to recognize moral ideals. It is simply not true that in urging a 'reluctant' person to do his duty we will be 'almost certain' to ask him: 'How would you like it if everyone did that?' Instead, we often appeal to such things as his sense of duty or his concern for others without ever asking this question.

In giving his account of the relationships between the two moralities, the author uses the figure of a sliding scale:

As we consider the whole range of moral issues, we may conveniently imagine a kind of scale or yardstick which begins at the bottom with the most obvious demands of social living and extends upward to the highest reaches of human aspiration. Somewhere along this scale there is an invisible pointer that marks the dividing line where the pressure of duty leaves off and the challenge of excellence begins. The whole field of moral argument is dominated by a great undeclared war over the location of this pointer. There are those who struggle to push it upward; others work to pull it down (pp. 9–10).

The author does not consider how the relationships between his two moralities might be misleadingly represented in the foregoing 'scale-model'. The model does suggest that the relation of duty to aspiration is one of simple arithmetic progression: 'a bit more is all the better'. But consider a father's duty to support and educate his child. In specific cases he may go beyond his duty and be

[1] For a useful discussion of the question 'Why should I be moral?', see FRANCIS HERBERT BRADLEY, ETHICAL STUDIES 58 (2nd ed., 1927).

virtuously generous—but if he goes too far his generosity will become foolishness and he will risk spoiling his child.[1] Second, many moral duties and moral aspirations do not stand in any sort of mutually consistent relation at all. In fact, they often conflict. Thus a utilitarian morality of aspiration may dictate disregard of some duties of popular morality.[2] Third, the author's model suggests that for each of our moral aspirations there is some corresponding duty or duties lower down the scale. But this is untrue. We may speak of justice and the duty to be just, but not of freedom and the duty to be free. Fourth, and conversely, there is not, for many of our moral duties, a corresponding moral aspiration or aspirations. How, for example, are we to think of such duties as the duty not to fornicate or the duty not to steal? These are not scaler concepts. There can be no higher and lower about them at all. One either fornicates or not. One either steals or not. Fifth, it is quite wrong to say that the whole field of moral argument is dominated by a great undeclared war over the location of a pointer marking the dividing line between duty and aspiration. There are other basic moral issues equally important and controversial: What should our *prima facie* duties be? How should moral conflicts be resolved? Which view of the good life is right?

## C. *Utility of the Distinction Between Moral Duties and Moral Aspirations*

Many scholars who discuss law and morality attempt, at some point, to compare and contrast the whole of morality with the whole of law. For this general purpose, the author's distinction between moral duties and moral aspirations is useful. It provides a partial inventory of the elements of morality, just as distinctions between types of 'directives' having authoritative force in a system of law provide a partial inventory of the elements of law. Without such inventories, some of the possible points of comparison between law and morality could not be satisfactorily considered; indeed, they might be overlooked entirely. We saw, however, that

[1] Cf. Chopra, *Professor Urmson on Saints and Heroes* 38 PHILOSOPHY 160, 164 (1963).
[2] This is one of the themes in the recent debates in Britain over the report of the Wolfenden Committee on Homosexual Offences and Prostitution. See *infra*, note 38.

the author's own efforts to clarify the distinction between moral duties and moral aspirations are not beyond criticism.

The author thinks his distinction also equips us to clarify social problems. And he thinks it of value to see just which of his two moralities contributes to the solution of social problems, though he does not say why. Some of the problems he has in mind are as follows:

1. Where should the line be drawn between that which should be our duty and that for which we should merely aspire? As we have seen, this is a big question for the author, and we should let him speak for himself:

If the morality of duty reaches upward beyond its proper sphere the iron hand of imposed obligation may stifle experiment, inspiration, and spontaneity. If the morality of aspiration invades the province of duty, men may begin to weigh and qualify their obligations, by standards of their own and we may end with the poet tossing his wife into the river in the belief—perhaps quite justified—that he will be able to write better poetry in her absence (pp. 27–8).

You will recall how in my first chapter I invoked the analogy of a kind of scale, starting at the bottom with the duties most obviously necessary to social existence and ending at the top with the highest and most difficult achievements of which human beings are capable. I also spoke of an invisible pointer as marking the line where the pressure of duty leaves off and the challenge of excellence begins. I regarded the proper location of that pointer as a basic problem of social philosophy. If it is set too low, the notion of duty itself may disintegrate under the influence of modes of thought appropriate only to the higher levels of a morality of aspiration. If the pointer is set too high, the rigidities of duty may reach up to smother the urge toward excellence and substitute for truly effective action a routine of obligatory acts (p. 170).

In the foregoing passages, the author misconceives the nature of morality. It is true that there are moralists who seem to want to make everything our duty. And there are others who think we have more than enough duties. But morality itself is not subject to change by determinate persons or groups. The notion of 'moral reform' is at least faintly absurd. We can reform laws, but not moral codes. In the realm of law, we do have legislators to 'set the pointer', but there are no moral legislators. Furthermore, even if there were, the author's definition of the problem would have

to be revised before these legislators could get to work. His definition at least implies that each and every duty can be shifted upward
or downward in some way, and we have seen that this is not so.[1] It
also suggests a picture of blanket duties that are uniformly
adjustable. Yet, not everyone has the same moral duties. And of
those duties that we may have in common, what constitutes their
performance varies from person to person. Consider the important
duty of parental support. A rich man would not discharge his duty
to his children by giving them only what the poorest man in the
community gave his children.

2. What holds society together? In response to this question, the
author seems to say two conflicting things. He says that the 'social
bond' in most societies rests on the 'reciprocity implicit in the
very notion of duty' (pp. 20–1). Later, at the end of his book, he
suggests that what holds society together is communication and
that the morality of aspiration enjoins us to keep the channels of
communication open (pp. 185–6). Without trying to reconcile
what is at least an apparent inconsistency, we may consider what
plausibility there is in the author's suggestion that society is held
together by a pervasive bond of reciprocity. First, what does it
mean to say a 'society is held together'? The author does not
elucidate this phrase. Is it enough to have a geographically
proximate group of persons who generally do their duties to each
other? If so, then it is plain that there are many reasons why
particular persons may do their duties other than or in addition
to the fact that they expect tacitly or openly, directly or indirectly,
some reciprocation. Such reasons include: habit, fear, desire for
respect, expectations of reward, and devotion to duty as such.
However, if no reciprocation were expectable at all, the group
might disintegrate. We cannot say.[2]

3. What conduct ought to be prohibited by law? The author
thinks it is the morality of duty that helps us answer this question:

There is no way by which the law can compel a man to live up to the
excellences of which he is capable. For workable standards of judgment
the law must turn to its blood cousin, the morality of duty. There, if

---

[1] See text following note 33, *supra*.

[2] The best discussion the writer has found of what might be called the role of
reciprocity in moral life is in Strawson, *Social Morality and the Individual Ideal*,
36 PHILOSOPHY 1 (1961). Sociologists and anthropologists have also studied this
phenomenon. See especially Gouldner, *The Norm of Reciprocity*, 25 AM. SOCIO.
REV. 161 (1960), and the many citations therein.

anywhere, it will find help in deciding whether . . . [conduct] . . . ought to be legally prohibited (p. 9).

But what does the author mean? If he means that we are to take the accepted morality of duty at its face value, then we can imagine that the foreoing passage would make Bentham fall off his chair.[1] For there is likely to be something irrational in every society's accepted morality of duty. It seems more likely that the author intends that we should turn for guidance not to the accepted morality of duty but to some form of 'critical' morality of duty.[2] And will even this provide 'workable standards'? Perhaps so and perhaps not. From the fact that conduct is 'so harmful that we ought to consider that there is a general moral duty, incumbent on all, to refrain from engaging in it' (p. 7), it does not follow that legal prohibitions against such conduct would be either proper or workable. We may, even with justification, morally condemn, but whether we should go further and legally proscribe is quite a different matter. This, above all else, has been established in the recent debates on the enforcement of morals to which the author refers (p. 133).[3]

4. What is the nature of law? The author claims that his distinction between the two moralities helps us clarify the nature of law. Whether this is so cannot be considered until after we have presented his theory of law.[4]

## II. THE NATURE OF THE LAW

We have divided this section into two parts. In the first, the author's theory of law is set forth. In the second, we measure his

[1] But not turn over in his grave. In fact, the writer saw Bentham recently. He is not in a grave at all, but, as per instructions in his will, is sitting on a chair inside a glass case at University College, London University.

[2] See generally, Urmson, *supra* note 16.

[3] The author there says he has found this debate 'quite inconclusive on both sides, resting as it does on initial assumptions that are not made explicit in the argument itself'. He then goes on to say he would not make private homosexual conduct between consenting adults criminal because such a law could not be enforced and would invite blackmail. But the author seems not to have done his homework. These considerations have been made explicit in the debate. See particularly, Hart, *The Use and Abuse of Criminal Law*, 4 OXFORD LAWYER 7 (1961).

[4] One further use the author says his distinction has we have relegated to footnote status. At p. 13, the author says the 'much debated question of the relation between fact and value would, I believe, be clarified if the disputants took pains to keep in mind the distinction between the moralities of duty and of aspiration'. However, what follows this remark is obscure.

theory against standards of criticism typically applied to theories of law.

## A. The Author's Theory of Law

The author sums up his theory as follows:

The only formula that might be called a definition of law offered in these writings is by now thoroughly familiar: law is the enterprise of subjecting human conduct to the governance of rules. Unlike most modern theories of law, this view treats law as an activity and regards a legal system as the product of a sustained purposive effort (p. 106).

In summary of the view I have advanced I may repeat that I have tried to see law as a purposive activity, typically attended by certain difficulties that it must surmount if it is to succeed in attaining its ends (p. 118).

The 'difficulties' to which the author refers really turn out to be the heart of his theory. Thus he opens his second chapter with an allegory in which he aptly illustrates 'eight ways to fail to make law'. We cannot do justice to the richness and complexity of his analysis within the confines of a review-article; instead, we shall have to be content with brief quotations. The author summarizes his eight ways to fail to make law as follows:

The first and most obvious lies in a failure to achieve rules at all, so that every issue must be decided on an ad hoc basis. The other routes are: (2) a failure to publicize, or at least to make available to the affected party, the rules he is expected to observe; (3) the abuse of retroactive legislation, which not only cannot itself guide action, but undercuts the integrity of rules prospective in effect, since it puts them under the threat of retrospective change; (4) a failure to make rules understandable (5) the enactment of contradictory rules or (6) rules that require conduct beyond the powers of the affected party; (7) introducing such frequent changes in the rules that the subject cannot orient his action by them; and finally, (8) a failure of congruence between the rules as announced and their actual administration. . . . A total failure in any one of these eight directions does not simply result in a bad system of law; it results in something that is not properly called a legal system at all . . . (p. 39).

The foregoing eight ways to fail to make law can be inversely formulated as eight requirements for social control through law.

As reformulated, the author often calls them 'elements' or 'principles' of legality. Further, he says:

All of them are means toward a single end, and under varying circumstances the optimum marshalling of these means may change. Thus an inadvertent departure from one desideratum may require a compensating departure from another; this is the case where a failure to give adequate publicity to a new requirement of form may demand for its cure a retrospective statute. At other times, a neglect of one desideratum may throw an added burden on another; thus, where laws change frequently, the requirement of publicity becomes increasingly stringent. In other words, under varying circumstances the elements of legality must be combined and recombined in accordance with something like an economic calculation that will suit them to the instant case (p. 104).

Does the author consider his theory to be a definition of law? He seems to. He also says he is specifying the 'conditions under which the ideal of "the rule of law" can be realized' (p. 39). He says, too, that 'What I have tried to do is to discern and articulate the natural laws of a particular kind of human undertaking . . .' (p. 96). Some readers may prefer to say he has tried to specify what laws must be like and how they must be administered for social control through law to achieve maximum effectiveness.

But regardless how we characterize in general terms what the author is up to, several specific features of his analysis should be underscored. First, he stresses what law is *for* rather than what law *is*. Indeed, he would object to this way of putting it, for he would say we cannot understand law at all unless we see what it is for. He attributes to law what he calls a 'modest and sober' aim: '. . . . that of subjecting human conduct to the guidance and control of general rules' (p. 146). This way of looking at social phenomena will remind readers of early Greek teleology, and more recently, of Von Jehring's *Law as a Means to an End*. Second, the author's analysis is 'process oriented'.[1] He works with a moving picture camera rather than a 'still' camera. He is interested in law as an activity—in physiology rather than anatomy.[2]

---

[1] A plea for more process-oriented philosophizing is made in Rescher, *Revolt Against Process* 59 J. PHIL. 410 (1962).

[2] By looking at law in this way, it is not so likely that, for example, such a basic feature of law as 'process ideals' will be overlooked. Such ideals tell us *how* law making and law administering activities ought to be conducted. One example is the ideal that statutes ought to be interpreted in accordance with their purposes.

Third, his theory is not only physiological but also, and quite naturally, pathological in emphasis. As we have seen, he introduces his theory via an account of 'eight ways to fail to make law'. This pathological orientation is compatible with the idealism that pervades his analysis, for one of the best ways to elaborate ideals is via their 'opposites'. Fourth, though idealism pervades his analysis, it is not a 'substantive' idealism. Instead it is procedural. Perhaps 'technological' is an even better word.[1] He has '. . . . nothing to say on such topics as polygamy, the study of Marx, the worship of God, the progressive income tax, or the subjugation of women' (p. 96). Instead, his interest is in the 'natural laws' of 'forms of social order'. Since law is one form of social order, we are to consider what '. . . institutional forms and practices [are] appropriate to its peculiar aims and problems' (p. 120). This theme, too, has Greek origins.[2] Finally, his theory is one of great *practical*

[1] See D'Entreves, *The Case for Natural Law Re-Examined* 1 NATURAL L.F. 5, 31 (1956).

[2] See the pseudo-Platonic dialogue: Plato, *Minos*, in LOEB CLASSICAL LIBRARY, PLATO: WITH AN ENGLISH TRANSLATION, Vol. 8, pp. 403–7 (Lamb transl. 1927):
. . . Soc. And do doctors on their part, in their treatises on health, write what they accept as real?
Com.   Yes.
Soc.   Then these treatises of the doctors are medical, and medical laws.
Com.   Medical, to be sure.
Soc.   And are agricultural treatises likewise agricultural laws?
Com.   Yes.
Soc.   And whose are the treatises and accepted rules about garden work?
Com.   Gardeners.
Soc.   So these are our gardening laws.
Com.   Yes.
Soc.   Of people who know how to control gardens?
Com.   Certainly . . .
Soc.   And whose are the treatises and accepted rules about the confection of tasty dishes?
Com.   Cooks.
Soc.   Then there are laws of cookery?
Com.   Of cookery.
Soc.   Of people who know, it would seem, how to control the confection of tasty dishes?
Com.   Yes . . .
Soc.   Very well; and now, whose are the treatises and accepted rules about the government of a state? Of the people who know how to control states are they not?
Com.   I agree. . . .
Soc.   Then we rightly admitted that law is discovery of reality?
Com.   So it appears. . . .
See generally, Chroust, *An Anonymous Treatise on Law: The Pseudo-Platonic Dialogue Minos*, 23 NOTRE DAME L. 47 (1947).

relevance. 'How can we maximize the efficiency of law?' is undeniably a practical question, and the author's thoughtful consideration of it is undeniably important.

## B. Critical Commentary

Yet as a theory of law, many readers will find what the author says unsatisfactory. He is obviously grinding an axe, and such emphasis inevitably distorts. Our first task, then, will be to identify distortions in his theory. But we would not want anyone to think we are against axe-grinding as such. We have ground many.[1] Second, we will show how the author fails to account for some fundamental ways to fail to make law. Third, we will evaluate the 'differentiating power' of his theory.

### 1. How does the author's theory distort the reality of law?

Theories of law typically distort in two ways. Either they overstress or they neglect some feature or aspect of law. These two vices are related, for the first often leads to the second. This is precisely what we have with the author's emphasis on purpose. In fixing on purpose in the way he does, he incapacitates his theory, for much of the reality of law cannot be represented in terms of purpose.

Nowhere does the author clarify the notion of purpose.[2] Yet it

---

[1] And of both types. Halfway, Oregon is a small place, and there are those of us who love it, with all its pine trees and bushes and other things requiring axework. He who would trade axe for pen, particularly to write about legal philosophy, is condemned always to look back with wistful eye.

[2] The best discussions we have found are as follows: Sparshott, *The Concept of Purpose*, 72 ETHICS 157, 164, 166 (1962), who says (1): 'For I think we are bound to say that we do not normally say that a person has a purpose unless he knows he has it, that the phrase "an unconscious purpose" has a "paradoxical ring to it" ', and (2) 'In speaking of purposes one is not speaking of the forces determining the conduct of an individual'; DOROTHY MARY EMMET, FUNCTION, PURPOSE AND POWERS 111 (1958) who says: 'When appealing to "purpose" it should be possible to say who is believed to be acting intentionally, and what specific end he is believed to be pursuing'; Laird, *It All Depends Upon the Purpose*, 1 ANALYSIS 49, 50–1 (1934) who says, 'In the great majority of instances . . . it is plain that in important senses, much does *not* "depend" on purpose. It does not depend on purpose that a purpose is what it is (i.e., has the characteristics it does have). Even if certain purposes are made subordinate by institution, it is usually the case that the subordination depends on the nature of the facts. It is seldom the case that the relation of means and end, or again, of proximate and ulterior purpose is itself the child of purpose; for its parents, usually, are time and circumstances'; Taylor, *Purposeful and Non-Purposeful*

is central to *The Morality of Law*. Purpose enters the author's picture of law in two ways. First, he says law is the 'purposive human enterprise of subjecting human conduct to the guidance and control of general rules'. This is to attribute a very general purpose to law as a whole. Secondly, the author, in many parts of his book, implicitly, and sometimes explicitly, assumes that the realities of law can be satisfactorily represented in terms of particular officials and citizens acting with specific purposes in mind.

What is there in the reality of law that cannot be readily accommodated within the author's 'purposive picture'? First, this picture leaves out of account the teachings of the so-called 'historical school' of legal philosophers. Montesquieu, Savigny, Maine, Vinogradoff, and others taught that we should not, in formulating theories of law, neglect such factors as custom, 'the spirit of the people', and even climate and geography. Though the excesses of these thinkers may be obvious enough, it does not follow that their most fundamental insight can be ignored. This insight was simply that some things cannot be satisfactorily understood unless we see how they have come to be. It may be open to 'analytical jurists' to say, simply, that such an insight is of little relevance to their 'structural' inquiries. But it is not open to the author to say this, for he purports to represent law as an activity—as a process.[1] He must therefore forge a conceptual framework the terminology of which will enable him to represent this activity faithfully. The terminology of purpose cannot represent many aspects of law stressed by historical jurists. Take custom, for example. Custom cannot be plausibly analyzed in terms of specific purposes of particular persons. Yet it is very much a part of law.

One of the insights of the historical jurists was that nonhuman elements permeate the law. Such elements cannot, by their very nature, be represented in terms of anyone's purposes. Even some human elements in the law cannot be represented in this way. Thus some 'legal realists' taught that law, which is not

[1] Cf. Strawson, *supra* note 16, at 14: 'Where what we are dealing with is a developing human institution, it is no reproach to an explanation that it may be described as at least partly genetic.'

---

*Behavior: A Rejoinder*, 17 PHIL. OF SCI. 327, 328 (1950) who says: 'Now I submit that, from observable behavior alone, one cannot certainly determine what the purpose of a behaving object is, nor indeed, whether it is purposeful at all'; and Nakhnikian, *Professor Fuller on Legal Rules and Purpose*, 2 WAYNE L. REV. 190, 197, (1956) who says that a purpose is 'no more a fact, than a pencil is'.

self-defining, must be interpreted and applied by determinate persons who are not always aware of the forces that influence them or do not always know their own minds. 'Purpose' cannot help us account for this aspect of law. One way to try to meet this point is to say that judges have 'unconscious purposes'. But the concept of unconscious purpose is an absurdity.

So-called 'acts in the law', e.g., wills, contracts, gifts, and even legislation, are a fundamental feature of all developed legal systems. A legal theory—a theory purporting to provide a conceptual framework the terminology of which is to be used to represent the reality of law in particular systems—must account for acts in the law. But the author's theory cannot satisfactorily do this. Consider contracts. Purposes are almost completely irrelevant to the formation of contracts in Anglo-American law. The objective theory of contract formation has been with us for a long while. Consider legislation as a second example. In Anglo-American law, the validity of legislation does not necessarily depend on anyone's purposes. Instead, it typically depends on compliance with established procedures.

A theory of law should also provide an account of legal sovereignty. But the author's theory does not. Furthermore, his theory of law as a purposive phenomenon cannot begin to account for the complex factors that influence compliance with the system. According to one whole tradition in legal thought, this compliance is to be represented in terms of 'habit',[1] a conception wholly at odds with 'purpose'. The habit theorists may have been wrong, but not wholly wrong.[2]

One reason the author embraces purpose to the extent he does is that he thinks much bad statutory interpretation can be traced to the failure of judges to peek at the purposes of legislators. Now we may agree that judges *ought* to heed legislators' purposes. But axe-grinding is one thing and providing a general theory of law is another. And we must not forget that in some legal systems judges have not been allowed to investigate the background of legislation.

[1] See JOHN AUSTIN, THE PROVINCE OF JURISPRUDENCE DETERMINED AND THE USES OF THE STUDY OF JURISPRUDENCE (Hart ed., 1954).

[2] In his discussions of the 'foundations' of legal systems, the author (and many others as well) does not always separate the following questions: (1) What criteria of legal validity are in fact applied in the system? (2) Why do citizens and officials use or go along with the use of these criteria?

To turn away from purpose and its inadequacies, another basic source of distortion in the author's theory of law is that he neglects what is sometimes called the 'structural' aspect of law. Indeed, he dismisses out of hand the whole tradition of legal thinkers who have sought to account for the structural complexities of law.[1] Surely these thinkers, including such incisive minds as Austin and Kelsen, were getting at something worth worrying about. A body does have an anatomy. And the anatomy of law is very complex, particularly in the developed legal systems of modern industrial societies. What constitutes 'legal validity'? How is it to be determined? What are the various 'sources of law' and what are their inter-relations? What significant differences are there between the various types of 'directives' having authoritative force in developed systems of law? What are the different functions of these directives? Can some be singled out as primary, and if so, in what sense? Such questions the author almost wholly neglects. This is not only to put to one side a whole tradition of legal philosophy, but also to close one's eyes to a very real aspect of the phenomena of law.

The author neglects a third fundamental dimension of law. He says:

Most theories of law either explicitly assert, or tacitly assume, that a distinguishing mark of law consists in the use of coercion or force. That distinguishing mark is not recognized in this volume (p. 108).

But from the fact that force is not a 'distinguishing feature of law' (assuming it is not), it does not follow that the author's force theorists have been worrying about unimportant problems. Yet the author implies as much. Indeed, he says:

Just what is meant by force when it is taken as the identifying mark of law? If in a theocratic society the threat of hell-fire suffices to secure obedience to its laws, is this 'a threat of force'? If so, then force begins to take on a new meaning and simply indicates that a legal system, to be properly called such has to achieve some minimum efficacy in practical affairs, whatever the basis of that efficacy—a proposition both unobjectionable and quite unexciting (pp. 109–10).

Surely a simple one-sentence solution to a problem that has puzzled many brilliant minds must inevitably fail. The whole of legal philosophy can be said to be concerned with law and morality and law and coercion. It may, therefore, startle more

[1] See pp. 110–18.

than a few scholars that the author is ready to lop off that whole branch concerned with the relations between law and coercion. The lay citizen will also be startled, for he commonly associates law with force. But what is meant by 'force'? Are force and coercion the same? What is the relationship between these concepts and the concept as well as the fact of obedience to law? In what specific ways is the layman's identification of law and force erroneous? Could law get along without force or coercion of some kind? And what is meant by 'minimum efficacy in practical affairs'? The author does not take such questions seriously. For he is not really interested in them. His is a different axe. He stresses how we *ought* to look at law, if we are to be most successful with it. His is the viewpoint of the engineer rather than the viewpoint of the armchair theorist. And however much readers will sympathize with his exhortations (as do we), many will be quick to see that even the enlightened engineer's vision is inevitably restricted.

### 2. *Is the author's pathology incomplete?*

The author, we saw, identifies eight ways to fail to make law. And he obviously thinks these eight have some special claim to comprehensiveness. But in fact they do not. There are other ways to fail to make law that are equally if not more fundamental than any of the ways the author identifies. First, his eight ways do not allow for the failure of a society to establish *authoritative* law-making procedures at the outset. The author does admit that a legal system must establish 'some minimum efficacy in practical affairs' (p. 110). But he cannot fit this factor into any one of his eight ways, and does not try. Instead, he presupposes such 'minimum efficacy'. Of course, the failure to establish authority may be pathologically insignificant in many Western societies; but it is not so everywhere.

Second, the author cannot, within his eight ways, satisfactorily accommodate failures to comply with authoritative law-making procedures after they have been set up. Late in the book, long after he has introduced and discussed his eight ways, the author does say of basic law-making procedures that: 'These rules . . . may meet shipwreck in all of the eight ways open to any system of law' (p. 148). But this seems to be an afterthought. The author, in almost every part of his discussion of the eight ways, presupposes the existence of established law-making procedures that have themselves been observed. In fact, he says the point of view he adopts is that of a legislator whose task is to subject human conduct to social control.[1] This point of view and this task sound not of fundamental law-making procedures, but of laws designed to control conduct at the stage of 'primary reliance'. It may be objected that the eighth of the author's eight ways—failure of congruence between rules and official action—specifically encompasses failure to comply with basic law-making procedures. Of course, it could be so stretched. But in his discussion of this eighth factor, the author says nothing of non-compliance with fundamental law-making procedures, and it is clear that he has devised this 'category' to accommodate ordinary garden variety situations in which officials fail to administer *admitted* laws 'congruently'.

So, law is not self-creating, and the author's pathology does not account for 'failures of creation'. But it is also true that law is not self-defining. For this reason, a third and no less important way to 'fail to make law' is to fail to provide institutions for the authoritative interpretation of law. It will not do just to 'make' law—to formulate it authoritatively. Institutions must be provided to tell us what it means in concrete situations. In modern legal systems, courts are the chief 'interpreters' of the law.[2] The failure to provide courts cannot, without distortion, be squeezed into any of the author's eight ways to fail to make law. Nowhere does he explicitly consider the necessity for courts; instead, he presupposes their existence.

Law is not self-creating, and it is not self-defining. It is also neither self-executing nor self-starting. Thus a fourth significant way to fail to make law—effective law—is to fail to provide for its

---

[1] Fixing on a restricted point of view is but one of many sources of error in legal philosophy. To name a few others: the influence of irrelevant or misleading models, e.g., the criminal law; the failure to see law as a dynamic rather than as a static affair; the quest for generality and universality; the desire for order and the influence of the reductionist impulse; the failure to separate conceptual questions from straightforward questions of fact; and axe-grinding. The literature of legal philosophy awaits a comprehensive analysis of such afflictions.

[2] Of course, there are other reasons why courts are needed. John Locke once said: 'In the State of Nature there wants a known and indifferent Judge, with Authority to determine all differences according to the established Law. For everyone in that state being both Judge and Executioner of the Law of Nature, Men being partial to themselves, Passion and Revenge is very apt to carry them too far, and with too much heat, in their own causes; as well as negligence, and unconcernedness, to make them too remiss in other Men's.' See PETER LASLETT, LOCKE'S TWO TREATISES OF GOVERNMENT 369 (1960).

execution by public official or private citizen. And it is not even enough to empower someone to execute the law. Steps must also be taken to assure that whoever is authorized to execute it will be motivated to do so.[1] Now this fourth way to fail to make law cannot be assimilated to any of the author's eight ways. He neglects it, presupposing that someone will put the law in motion.

These, then, are some, but only some,[2] of the ways that law can fail which must be added to the author's pathology. It might be objected that each is really irrelevant to the author, for he is only trying to identify those 'total failures' which do 'not simply result in a bad system [but] in something that is not properly called a legal system at all' (p. 39). But a total failure in any one of the 'directions' we have identified would produce 'something that is not properly called a legal system at all'. There can be no law without authoritative law-making procedures and institutions for the interpretation and enforcement of law. It might be objected that the author generally adopts the viewpoint of a legislator, and our additional 'four ways' cannot be subjected to legislative control. But it is not true that all of our additional 'factors of failure' cannot be subjected to legislative control. Anyway, the legislative viewpoint is too narrow. Finally, it may be objected that the author himself somewhere in his book considers or touches upon what we would add to his pathology. But even if this were true, it would be largely irrelevant, for the heart and core of the author's theory of law is, by his own admission, that law is a purposive human enterprise that can 'fail of its purpose' in the eight ways he identifies.

### 3. What is the 'differentiating power' of the author's analysis?

The extent to which a theory differentiates law from other social

---

[1] See Pound, *The Limits of Effective Legal Action*, 27 ETHICS 166 (1916). And see JEREMY BENTHAM, THE LIMITS OF JURISPRUDENCE DEFINED 230 (1945). It was Locke who also said: 'Where the laws cannot be executed, it is all one as if there were no Laws. . . .' LASLETT, op. cit., *supra* note 51, at 429.

[2] To distinguish and identify a few others: (1) The failure to provide effective remedies for noncompliance, (2) the failure to maintain the minimal socioeconomic conditions required for compliance, (3) a general failure to observe such essentials of 'natural justice' as judicial impartiality and a right to a hearing so that disrespect for law becomes common, (4) the use of law to control the uncontrollable, e.g., religious belief, love, and so on. See generally, CHARLES G. HOWARD and ROBERT S. SUMMERS, LAW, ITS NATURE, FUNCTIONS, AND LIMITS (1965), Ch. 16 and bibliography thereto. See also JEREMY BENTHAM, THE PRINCIPLES OF MORALS AND LEGISLATION 316–23 (1948 ed.).

phenomena is one standard jurists always apply to evaluate theories of law. Judged by this standard, the author's theory fails. According to him, we have legal systems all over the place. Any purposive enterprise for ordering human relations through general rules is a legal system. The author is quite willing to live with this. He says:

At this point I am sure there will be those who, though agreeing generally with my negations and rejections, will nevertheless feel a certain discomfort about the view of law I have presented as my own. To them the concept of law that underlies these writings will seem too loose, too accommodating, too readily applied over too wide a range of instances to serve significantly as a distinctive way of looking at law (p. 118).

A view that seeks to understand law in terms of the activity that sustains it, instead of considering only the formal sources of its authority, may sometimes suggest a use of words that violates the normal expectations of language. This inconvenience may, I suggest, be offset by the capacity of such a view to make us perceive essential similarities. It may help us to see that the imperfectly achieved systems of law within a labor union or a university may often cut more deeply into the life of a man than any court judgment ever likely to be rendered against him. On the other hand, it may also help us to realize that all systems of law, big and little, are subject to the same infirmities. In no case can the legal achievement outrun the perception of the human beings who guide it. The judicial review of institutional disciplinary measures performs its most obvious service when it corrects outrageous injustice; in the long run it can be most useful if it helps to create an atmosphere within institutions and associations that will render it unnecessary (p. 129).

The foregoing passages show clearly that the author is at his axe, grinding it with abandon. It may be well for other 'forms of social order' to borrow some 'law-ways', but it certainly does not follow from this that unions and universities have legal systems—or, to put it the other way around, that law should be 'persuasively redefined'[1] to encompass all forms of control through rules.

### III. MORALITY AND LAW: CONTRASTS AND RELATIONSHIPS

We have considered the author's accounts of morality and of law. How are these phenomena to be related and contrasted? The

---

[1] See Stevenson, *Persuasive Definitions* 47 MIND 331 (1938) for discussion of this familiar phenomenon.

author's answer to this question can be sub-divided into the following parts: 'ordinary' morality and law; natural law and law; justice and law; and, the 'internal morality' of law.

## A. 'Ordinary' Morality and Law

The author, we saw, distinguishes between 'internal' and 'external' moralities of law. 'External' morality is morality in the ordinary, familiar sense. How does the author differentiate law from ordinary morality, consisting, as it does, of principles and conceptions of what is right and good? All he says is that law is the subject of an 'explicit responsibility' whereas morality is not (p. 130). In a book on morality and law, some readers might have hoped for a more detailed account. The questions to be considered in such an account would include: Are there any differences in the ways law and morality change? In the nature of the influences that affect legal and moral change? Are there any differences in the nature of the excuses allowed for moral wrongs and those allowed for legal wrongs? Are moral duties more *'prima facie'* than legal duties? How, if at all, do specifically moral sanctions differ from legal sanctions?[1] Do the components of morality differ from the components of legal systems? Is it appropriate to speak of a morality as a system? What differences are there between the ways in which moral and legal precepts are applied in practice? We speak of public and private morality but not of public and private legal systems. Why? We may speak of several moralities in one society, but not of several legal systems. Why? We may coerce the performance of legal duties without diminishing the value of this performance, but this is untrue of moral duties. Why? Do we compare different moral systems on points other than those on which we compare different legal systems? If so, why?

So much for contrasts. What are the relationships between ordinary morality and law? The author says the two interact—presumably, this means they affect the content of each other. But again, we might have expected a more detailed account, including at least tentative answers to such questions as: How does morality affect the administration of law? How and to what extent are law and morality mutually dependent?

[1] Professor Hart helpfully discusses several of these questions in H. L. A. HART, THE CONCEPT OF LAW 169–76 (1961).

## B. *Natural Law and Law*

Some think of natural law as a form of morality. Is the author's theory of law a natural law theory? The author answers this question with an emphatic though qualified 'yes' (p. 96). His eight forms of legal excellence he calls a 'procedural' natural law. His concern is '. . . not with the substantive aims of legal rules, but with the ways in which a system of rules for governing human conduct must be constructed and administered if it is to be efficacious and at the same time remain what it purports to be'.

Observe that this is not a traditional natural law theory,[1] for traditional theories are concerned with substantive ideals. Yet it is 'natural' in the sense that it draws upon characteristics of man and basic elements of the human condition of which we must be cognizant if man is to be controlled through general rules.

The author has an opportunity to endorse a more traditional—a more substantive—natural law theory at the end of his book, but he declines. Instead, he criticizes Professor H. L. A. Hart's substantive theory of natural law (pp. 184–5). One consequence is that the book leaves the reader in the dark as to precisely when, for the author, an evil law cannot be a law at all.[2]

## C. *Justice and Law*

Justice is both a moral ideal and a moral virtue. What does the author say about it and its relation to law? The first thing to notice is that the author's conception of law, which he describes as procedural in nature, cannot readily accommodate such elementary procedural principles—often called principles of natural justice— as that a judge shall not be a judge in his own cause, shall give each party a chance to be heard, and shall give reasons for his conclusions. These, surely, are ideals of the first order.

As for justice in the substantive sense, the author contents himself with two pages in which he stresses that his conception of law requires that 'officials act by known rule', which, he says, is a 'precondition for any meaningful appraisal of the justice of law' (pp. 157–9). Again, we might have hoped for a more detailed account.

---

[1] For an incisive recent critique of such theories, see Bobbio, *Quelques arguments contre le Droit Naturel* LE DROIT NATUREL (1959).

[2] See especially pp. 123 and 168.

## D. *The 'Internal Morality' of Law*

That legal rules should be general, clear, publicized, prospective, stable, 'congruently' administered, and within the capacity of citizens to obey, constitutes, for the author, what he calls the 'internal morality' of law. We saw that these desiderata may be thought of as the 'opposites' of his eight ways to fail to make law. If these in fact constitute a morality, then it is clear that law and morality are inextricably intertwined. For in most legal systems, we obviously cannot have anything resembling social control through law unless we have rules that are general, prospective, clear, and so on. Thus, on the author's analysis, morality pervades the whole legal enterprise. Now it is easy enough to show that the author's analysis turns on an extended use of the word 'morality'. But why should he want to extend this word? What axe is he grinding? The answer—or at least one answer—is reasonably clear. If law has an internal morality, then this morality and the law itself cannot be separated, and 'positivistic' efforts to separate them are not just difficult but are fundamentally misconceived. It would be possible to show that the author here jousts at windmills, for at least some of his opponents would not deny that if we are to have law at all, we must have some compliance with the author's 'principles of legality'. They do deny that these principles constitute a 'morality', or are even moral in nature.

What are the author's reasons for calling his principles of legality a morality? On page 168 of his book—sixteen pages into the last chapter—he says: 'So far in this chapter I have attempted to show that the internal morality of law does indeed deserve to be called a "morality" '. To some readers, this sentence will come as a shock, for the author has not, in advance, told them what he was up to. When we turn back we find four arguments that he is apparently advancing to support the proposition that his 'internal morality' is a morality. First, he argues that his internal morality is a morality because only through it can we achieve substantively moral laws: 'Law is a pre-condition of good law' (p. 155). But the obvious answer to this is that law can be used for bad as well as good ends. When used for bad ends, what are we to say? 'Laws used in this way are in a sense moral but in another sense immoral?' This is but one of the things the author's analysis demands, but observe how confusing it is likely to be to the citizen. Implicit in this first argument

is also the assumption that anything conducive to good law deserves
to be considered part of the internal morality of law. But what of
West Publishing Co.? There are some who would say that without
West the whole system would collapse. Are we therefore to say
that West, with its reporting system, and its helpful organizing
categories, constitutes part of the inner morality of law? And
what of the principles of clear draftsmanship appearing in the
handbooks? On the author's analysis, we have no way of keeping
these, and much else, from being swept into the moral category.

Second, the author argues that the three requirements of
generality, publicity, and congruent administration tend to assure
morally good laws. For example, he says a 'rule articulated and
made known permits the public to judge of its fairness' (p. 159).
Now we may agree that officials are more likely to behave respon-
sibly if their actions are publicized. But, what may tend to secure
moral goodness is surely not by itself moral. Many things, including wealth and literacy, tend to assure moral goodness but they
are not themselves moral. Third, the author argues that the
'internal' requirement of clarity is a moral principle, for some
evil aims simply cannot be clearly articulated in laws (pp. 157–
62). But there is no correlation whatsoever between clarity of
formulation and goodness. Many good aims are as difficult to
formulate in statutes as are some bad aims, and some bad aims
are as easy to formulate in statutes as many good ones. Fourth,
and finally, the author makes a very general argument that his
internal morality is a true morality because 'implicit' in it is a view
of man 'as a responsible agent' (p. 162). Now this argument really
proves far too much. According to it, any form of ordering that
assumes man's actions are 'responsible' deserves to be called a
morality. Thus we sweep in rules of etiquette, rules of games, the
operating procedures of corporations, unions, and so on.

The author's own case for calling his principles of legality a
*morality* is weak. And there are still more counter arguments. We
normally think of a morality or a moral code as consisting of
substantive rather than procedural ideals or principles. Yet the
author's analysis must accommodate such strange bedfellows as
chastity and the avoidance of contradiction. Furthermore, for
most of us there is a very close connection between our moral
principles and actual human good. We think such good comes from
compliance with these principles, and we demand justification for

any departure from them. Accordingly, with us, it would be highly paradoxical if these principles could be inverted and yet reamin of positive moral value. Thus, it would be thought absurd to speak of embarking upon a general program of stealing or lying 'in the interest of human goodness'. But it is not the same with the author's eight principles of legality. In fact, we might determine that in some spheres compliance with them would be bad. Indeed, the author himself says that we may, in order to do good, have to embark upon a *policy* of retroactive legislation. Similarly, we may decline to formulate general rules as a matter of policy, hoping thereby to determine more freely what course ultimately to take. A further reason for refusing to apply the halo word 'morality' to the author's principles of legality is that there is an apposite alternative: They may be viewed as 'maxims of legal efficacy' and maxims of this nature are not, as such, conceptually connected with morality. If a person assembles a machine inefficiently, the result is inefficiency, not immorality.

Having rejected the author's analysis, it may be worthwhile to try to show just how morality does enter the picture. Let us assume that the author's imaginary king 'Rex' failed in all the author's eight ways to make law (pp. 33–8). We would certainly say his conduct violated moral principles. There is a moral principle that the authority of man over man is not to be abused. There is also a moral principle that public officials should faithfully discharge the public trust.[1] Also relevant are such principles as that it is man's duty to be just and his duty not to be cruel. Thus when the author's imaginary king punishes, for example, a citizen who has not 'complied' with a retroactive secret statute, he violates all the foregoing, and perhaps other, moral principles. But this does not warrant our calling the 'demands' of clarity, generality, prospectiveness, and so on, moral principles. However, we think we can see why someone might want to speak of an internal morality of law. Very often, when we use 'ought' we use it morally, and each of the author's eight desiderata can be phrased in terms of 'ought'; that is, we may say laws ought to be clear, ought to be prospective, and so on. This, alone, might not tempt anyone to say such 'oughts' are moral oughts. But when we add the fact that unclear or

---

[1] The trust conception is prominent in Locke. See LASLETT, op. cit. *supra* note 51, at 112, 301, 356, 381, 385, 399, 419, 422, 430, 437. See also Horsburgh, *The Ethics of Trust*, 10 THE PHILOSOPHICAL QUARTERLY 343 (1960).

retrospective laws sometimes violate moral principles, then we are more tempted to think of the author's desiderata as moral principles. This temptation must be resisted. A *way* to violate a moral principle is not itself a moral principle.[1] In the appropriate conditions and circumstances, we could violate a moral principle merely by looking out a window. But we should not be led by this to say that there is a moral principle against looking out windows.

## CONCLUSION

Insofar as this book is intended to establish an internal *morality* of law, it is a failure. But the book should not be judged a failure. It is the best discussion of the demands of the rule of law in existing literature. And, it establishes beyond doubt that compliance with 'principles of legality' is essential if we are to order our daily lives. It is filled, too, with many brilliant insights along the way. The book should be widely read.

[1] For the suggestion that a 'way' to violate a moral principle implicitly involves a derivative moral principle, see Harrison, *When is a Principle A Moral Principle?*, 28 (Supp. Vol.) PROCEEDINGS OF THE ARISTOTELIAN SOCIETY 111 (1954).

# Hart's Concept of Law

## ROLF SARTORIUS*

### I

H. L. A. Hart's *The Concept of Law*[1] is one of the most important contributions to analytic jurisprudence to have been made in the English language since Austin's *The Province of Jurisprudence Determined*, and my primary purpose in the present essay is to subject its central theses to a more detailed analysis than they have yet received by Hart's reviewers and other critics.[2] My aim will not only be to call attention to those points at which I believe Hart's analysis is unsatisfactory—this job has already been done quite admirably by others—but to attempt a more general diagnosis of the source of these difficulties in Hart's theory.

Before moving to what I hope will be both illuminating exposition as well as constructive criticism of the central claims put forward in *The Concept of Law*, I should first like to sketch a framework within which I believe such an examination can most fruitfully take place.

* Associate Professor of Philosophy, University of Minnesota. The essay reprinted here first appeared in 52 ARCHIV FUR RECHTS UND SOZIALPHILOSOPHIE 161 (1966).

[1] Oxford: Oxford University Press, 1961.

[2] Among the more important of the many discussions of Hart's book are, in my estimation, the following: Edgar Bodenheimer, *Review of Hart's Concept of Law* 10 UCLA LAW REVIEW 959 (1962); Jonathan L. Cohen, *Hart's Concept of Law* 71 MIND 395 (1962); LON FULLER, THE MORALITY OF LAW Ch. III (New Haven: Yale University Press, 1964); B. E. King, *The Basic Concept of Professor Hart's Jurisprudence: The Norm Out of the Bottle*, CAMBRIDGE LAW JOURNAL 270 (1963); Herbert Morris, *The Concept of Law-Review* 75 HARVARD LAW REVIEW 1452 (1962); Alf Ross, *Hart's Concept of Law-Review* 71 YALE LAW JOURNAL 1185 (1962); Marcus G. Singer, *Hart's Concept of Law* 60 JOURNAL OF PHILOSOPHY 197 (1963); Ronald Dworkin, *The Model of Rules* 35 UNIVERSITY OF CHICAGO LAW REVIEW 14 (1967).

II

It is obvious—but important, seldom denied—but often disregarded, that the question 'What is law?' is a paradigm of ambiguity.[1] Since I believe that Hart's views may be profitably examined in the light of the various forms which this question may take, I shall distinguish those forms of the question to which I believe Hart has directed himself in *The Concept of Law*. Employing this as my 'principle of disambiguation', it seems to me clear that the following forms of the question 'What is law?' must be distinguished: (1) 'What is a legal system?' (2) 'What is a valid law?'; (3) 'What is the essence, or nature, of law?'; (4) 'What is a good reason for a judicial decision?' Let me indicate briefly how I shall understand each of these questions throughout the remainder of this essay.

(1) 'What is a legal system?', as it has been traditionally understood, and as I shall construe it here, represents a request for a definition specifying a set of necessary and sufficient conditions for the existence of a legal system. Such a *real definition* of 'legal system' is viewed as being based upon and reflecting the pre-analytic meaning of that expression, and it is this which is said to distinguish it from a mere stipulation or convention—a *nominal definition*—as to the way in which 'legal system' is to be understood in a certain specified context.

(2) It seems an obvious truism that relative to any well-developed system of municipal law there is a distinction between those rules which are valid rules of law within the system and other rules which, though they may become laws, are not yet part of the law. Indeed, there is usually little difficulty in specifying the criteria which must be conformed with, or the legislative procedures which must be followed, if a non-legal rule is to become a valid law within any particular legal system. Within and relative to any legal system, it has thus been argued, there must be an ultimate criterion for the validity of what are recognized as rules of law within that system. And if every legal system must contain such an ultimate criterion of validity, it has been thought, perhaps such criteria—despite their important differences from system to system—will all satisfy certain general conditions which will then provide

---

[1] The only explicit attempt of which I am aware to disambiguate this question is Richard Wollheim, *The Nature of Law* 2 POLITICAL STUDIES 128 (1954).

a sort of meta-criterion for criteria of validity. As Professor Wollheim has put it:

... a criterion of legal validity is necessarily relative to a legal system; each system has its own criterion, and to ask for a criterion without specifying the system is analogous to asking for the method of scoring without specifying the game. But, it has been felt, perhaps what we can give is, not a general criterion of validity for all systems, but a *general schema for the criterion of validity of any system*; a skeleton, as it were, that any criterion must satisfy if it is to fulfill its proper task— just as we might hope to give, not a general method of scoring, but a schema that any method must satisfy.[1]

Such a general schema for criteria of validity would clearly be tantamount to a real definition of the expression 'valid law', for it would specify a set of conditions which are individually necessary and jointly sufficient for the correct application of this expression to a rule within any particular legal system. It is in just this way that the question 'What is a valid law?' has in fact been traditionally understood, and I shall continue to construe it in this manner —as does Hart—in what is to follow.

(3) 'What is *the* essence, or nature, of law?', if one is to judge by the answers which have been given to it, may be interpreted as calling for a description of *the* most important feature or features of a legal system. What, though, is to be understood by the claim that a particular feature of a legal system is *important*? Is importance, as Glanville Williams has claimed, merely a subjective and emotional matter?[2] It need not be. For the contention that a certain characteristic feature of municipal legal systems, C, is important, may be construed as an objective conceptual claim of the following sort. The legal philosopher is typically concerned with the elucidation (perhaps through real definition) of certain legal concepts, such as that of a legal system, a valid law, a legal right, sovereignty, etc. To the degree to which C provides an adequate basis upon which these concepts may be elucidated, C is *an* important feature of a legal system. The claim that a certain characteristic feature of municipal legal systems constitutes *the* essence or nature of law—'the key to the science of jurisprudence',

---

[1] Wollheim, op. cit., p. 132.

[2] Glanville Williams, *The Controversy Concerning the Word 'Law'* PHILOSOPHY, POLITICS AND SOCIETY 183 (Peter Laslett, ed., 1st series, Oxford: Basil Blackwell, 1956).

as Austin put it—amounts to no more and no less than the claim that this feature provides a basis upon which most if not all of the concepts with which the legal philosopher is concerned may be elucidated.

(4) Professor Dworkin writes: 'What, in general, is a good reason for decision by a court of law? This is *the* question of jurisprudence; it has been asked in an amazing number of forms, of which the classic "What is Law?" is only the briefest.'[1] Although I share Dworkin's interest in the nature of the justification of the judicial decision, I can agree neither that it is *the* question of jurisprudence, nor that 'What is law?' is but one form of the question 'What, in general, is a good reason for decision by a court of law?' The latter question, though, is one form which the former question has frequently taken, and although this question does not appear as of central concern to Hart in *The Concept of Law*, some of his primary theses quite clearly commit him to very definite views concerning at least some aspects of the nature of a good reason for a judicial decision.

While the four forms of the question 'What is law?' that have been enumerated above are clearly distinct from one another, it must be equally clear that there are close relationships among them. The relationships among these questions are—or at least appear to be—so close, in fact, that it should not be surprising that the relationships between the answers which a given legal philosopher gives to them may also be so close that they may be said to constitute a unified *theory* of law. John Austin's theory of sovereignty provides a familiar example.[2] Claiming to have found in the notions of a command and habitual obedience 'the key to the science of jurisprudence', Austin defined the sovereign in an independent political society as that determinate person (or group of persons) whose commands are habitually obeyed by the majority of the members of that society and who does not render habitual obedience to anyone else. A valid law, on this view, is simply an express or tacit command, general as to acts, directed by the sovereign to his subjects, and a judicial decision is said to be justified if and only if, given the legal facts of the case, it is deducible from one or

---

[1] Ronald Dworkin, *Wasserstrom: The Judicial Decision* 75 ETHICS 47 (October 1964).

[2] THE PROVINCE OF JURISPRUDENCE DETERMINED, Introduction by H. L. A. Hart (1954).

more valid laws. Finally, the necessary and sufficient condition for the existence of a legal system is the presence of an Austinian sovereign.

We have, then, delimited four forms of the question 'What is law?', and noted that a unified answer to these four questions, such as Austin's, may be said to constitute a philosophical theory of law. Keeping these questions in mind, we may now turn to our examination of Professor Hart's concept of law.

## III

There are grounds for some confusion as to just what answer Hart has given to the question 'What is law?' in *The Concept of Law*, and there are also reasons for some doubts as to which forms of this question he is attempting to answer. Perhaps it will thus be best to turn first to the answer; once we are confident what that is, we may be in a better position to determine the question or questions which it is meant to fit. It should be kept in mind from the outset, though, that Hart's analysis is offered as an alternative to, and in large part grows out of his criticisms of, the theory of John Austin. Since we have just seen that Austin's theory provided a comprehensive account of positive law in terms of which all four forms of the question 'What is law?' which we have distinguished are answered, we should not be surprised if Hart's treatment of the question has at least the appearance of being equally comprehensive.

The focal point of Hart's detailed and penetrating criticisms of Austin's theory in *The Concept of Law* is that

(t)he elements he (Austin) uses do not include the notion of a *rule* or the rule-dependent notion of what *ought* to be done; the notions of a *command* and a *habit* however ingeniously combined cannot yield them or take their place though Austin often uses the word 'rule' and defines it as a kind of command.[1]

It is on the basis of a distinction between two types of legal rules that Hart hopes to deal with the question 'What is law?' 'The main theme of this book', Hart tells us of *The Concept of Law*,

is that so many of the distinctive operations of the law, and so many of the ideas which constitute the framework of legal thought, require

[1] ibid., p. xii.

for their elucidation reference to one or both of these two types of rules, that their union may be justly regarded as the 'essence' of law, though they may not always be found together whenever the word 'law' is correctly used.[1]

The two types of rules the union of which Hart claims provides 'the key to the science of jurisprudence' which eluded Austin are labeled *primary* and *secondary* rules. Hart describes the distinction between them in these two ways:

(1) Rules of the first type impose duties; rules of the second type confer powers, public or private. Rules of the first type concern actions involving physical movement or change; rules of the second type provide for operations which lead not merely to physical movement or change, but to the creation or variation of duties or obligations.[2]

(2) . . . while primary rules are concerned with the actions that individuals must or must not do, . . . secondary rules are all concerned with the primary rules themselves. They specify the ways in which the primary rules may be conclusively ascertained, introduced, eliminated, varied, and the fact of their violation conclusively determined.[3]

The distinction made in (1) is the familiar (but not to my mind unproblematic) one between duty imposing rules and power conferring rules; what Alf Ross refers to as the distinction between norms of conduct and norms of competence.[4] In (2), the primary rules are again rules which impose duties, but the secondary rules are now confined to rules specifying 'the ways in which the primary rules may be conclusively ascertained, introduced, eliminated, varied, and the fact of their violation conclusively determined', i.e., the rules which Hart refers to respectively as the rules of recognition, change, and adjudication. Now the distinctions made by (1) and (2) are obviously different distinctions. According to (1), such laws as those governing marriages, wills, trusts, and contracts, all of which confer legal powers (or capacities) on private individuals, are secondary rules; according to (2), they are not. Not only will some of what are secondary rules according to (1) not be secondary rules according to (2), the converse will also hold. In particular, the rules of recognition which specify the authoritative sources of law, unlike the rules of change and adjudication, are not *necessarily* power conferring

---

[1] HART, THE CONCEPT OF LAW 151.　　　[2] ibid., p. 79.　　　[3] ibid., p. 92.
[4] ALF ROSS, ON LAW AND JUSTICE 32 (1959).

rules at all. As Professor Cohen has noted, they merely establish the criteria of legal validity which may, but need not, refer to legislative or judicial powers—specified in the rules of change—to make new laws and change old ones.

> The rules he calls rules of recognition are not rules that confer powers, whether public or private: they set up criteria. They determine the sources of law: they do not give power to someone to make it. . . . Sometimes, e.g., in the Roman-Dutch law of South Africa, a document or textbook which had little or no authority in a given community at the time it was written, or could have had no authority at all because the community scarcely existed, is later recognized by that community as an authoritative source of law. In such a case it borders on absurdity to suppose that the relevant rule of recognition constitutes a retroactive, and probably posthumous, grant of legislative powers to the author of the document or textbook.[1]

What, then, is the relevant distinction between primary and secondary rules? Is it that between rules which impose duties and those which confer powers? Or is it that between the constitutional rules of recognition, change and adjudication and all other sorts of legal rules? Or perhaps that between these constitutional rules and those rules which impose duties on private individuals? Or simply that between public and private law?[2] Or, finally, perhaps it is that between the rule of recognition alone and primary rules of obligation. Hart lends support to this latter interpretation when he writes of the 'complex social situation where a secondary rule of recognition is accepted and used for the identification of primary rules of obligation', that '(i)t is this situation which deserves, if anything does, to be called the foundations of a legal system'.[3]

While each one of these distinctions may be important in so far as it will illuminate a certain class of problems, it must be clear that no *one* of these distinctions will provide a basis for answering *all* of the questions in which Hart is interested, let alone all of those which are of legitimate concern to others. In this sense, then, there is simply no such thing as *the* distinction which we may understand

---

[1] Cohen, op. cit., p. 408.

[2] *Black's Law Dictionary* (3rd ed., 1933) defines private law: 'As used in contradistinction to public law, the term means all that part of the law which is administered between citizen and citizen, or which is concerned with the definition, regulation, and enforcement of rights in cases where both the person in whom the right inheres and the person upon whom the obligation is incident are private individuals.'  [3] HART, THE CONCEPT OF LAW 97.

Hart as having made between primary and secondary rules. In discussing some problems, Hart makes use of one form of this ambiguous distinction; in discussing other problems, he makes use of quite different forms of the distinction. And as will be shown in Section VI below, there are some points upon which even Hart himself puts very great emphasis to which the distinction between primary and secondary rules in *any* one of its forms seems to be either totally irrelevant or else completely unilluminating.

In spite of the above considerations, I believe that it is possible to isolate that form of the distinction between primary and secondary rules to which Hart in practice assigns the greatest weight. It is the somewhat hybrid distinction between the constitutional rules of recognition, change, and adjudication, on the one hand, and those rules which impose duties and confer powers upon private individuals, and which could exist independently of the secondary rules, on the other hand.¹ It is as understood in this way, I believe, that Hart wishes to claim that the addition of secondary rules to a set of pre-existing primary rules marks the (perhaps hypothetical) transition from the pre-legal into the legal world.² Although Hart is concerned with much else in *The Concept of Law*, I believe it is this transition which he is most intent upon describing.

Understanding the distinction between primary and secondary rules as it has been reformulated above, I believe that it is fair to say that Professor Hart's one sentence answer to the question 'What is law?' is: 'Law is the union of primary and secondary rules.' But this question, we have seen, admits of a variety of interpretations, and we must now seek to determine in which of its forms Hart is committed to answering it in terms of the union of primary and secondary rules.

IV

In spite of his frequent disclaimers to the contrary,³ it does often appear as if Hart is defending a particular definition of 'legal system':

---

¹ Rules for the regulation of the behavior of individuals may in some cases only be significant where there are also secondary rules which create courts. For example, the rules concerning the formation of certain kinds of trusts.
² HART, THE CONCEPT OF LAW 91 f.          ³ ibid., especially pp. 13–17.

There are therefore *two minimum conditions necessary and sufficient for the existence of a legal system.* On the one hand those rules of behavior which are valid according to the system's ultimate criteria of validity must be generally obeyed, and, on the other hand, its rules of recognition specifying the criteria of legal validity and its rules of change and adjudication must be effectively accepted as common public standards of official behavior by its officials.[1]

So long as the laws which are valid by the system's tests of validity are obeyed by the bulk of the population this surely is *all the evidence we need in order to establish that a given legal system exists.*[2]

Given such statements as these, it is not surprising that there have been those, such as Professor Singer, who have decided that there is 'nothing wrong with the conclusion that Hart has provided a definition of law'.[3] But there surely would be something wrong with concluding that statements such as these implicitly contain a definition of 'legal system', and this is because they constitute nothing more than *purely formal criteria* for the existence of a legal system. As such, they could be satisfied by the rules, officials, and players of the National Football League, as well as many other rule governed social organizations. And Professor Hart, who at one point notes that the definition of law and morals 'in purely formal terms, without reference to any specific content or social needs, has proved inadequate',[4] is certainly aware of this.

If one is intent upon extracting from Hart's analysis a *definition* of 'legal system', indeed, if one wants a complete picture of Hart's *concept* of law, one must put together (1) what is said about the union of primary and secondary rules with (2) what Hart argues is the minimal content of Natural Law shared by both law and morals, and then combine all of this with (3) what Hart claims are the four features of morality which distinguish it from law, custom, etiquette, and other kinds of systems of social rules. Let me expand briefly on this:

(1) The addition of secondary rules of recognition, change, and adjudication to a set of primary rules is, says Hart, 'a step forward as important to society as the invention of the wheel', and it is this step which Hart marks as 'the step from the pre-legal into the legal world'.[5] For the addition of a rule of recognition makes possible the

---

[1] ibid., p. 113 (italics mine).     [2] ibid., p. 111 (italics mine).
[3] Singer, op. cit., p. 200.     [4] HART, THE CONCEPT OF LAW 194.
[5] ibid., p. 41.

conclusive identification of the primary rules, and thus remedies the *uncertainty* inherent in a simple set of customary or conventional primary rules which exist alone. Similarly, the remedy for the *static* quality of a bare set of primary rules is the addition of rules of change which provide for the variation of old rules and the introduction of new ones. Lastly, rules of adjudication remedy the *inefficiency* of the means by which a simple set of primary rules must be enforced, for they provide for the other than private settlement (by courts) of disputes which arise under the primary rules.[1]

(2) Hart's 'minimal version' of Natural Law is to the effect that, given survival as an aim, it is a matter of *natural necessity* that there are certain rules of conduct which any social organization must enforce if it is to be viable. The *natural necessity* resides in the fact that there are certain obvious generalizations about man and the nature of the world in which he finds himself which constitute *good reasons* for both law and morals having a specific content. In particular, claims Hart, as long as these generalizations remain true, any viable social organization must provide some minimal protection of persons, property, and promises through a system of mutual forbearances enforced by sanctions, the latter being required 'not as the normal motive for obedience, but as a *guarantee* that those who would voluntarily obey shall not be sacrificed to those who would not'.[2]

(3) Although many forms of rule governed social organization might be formally regarded as presenting a union of primary and secondary rules, it is clear that the rules of an organization like the National Football League do not have the content which according to Hart's minimal version of Natural Law any legal system must have as a matter of natural necessity. What is easily conceivable, though, is a *moral code* having both the form of a union of primary and secondary rules as well as the minimal content demanded by Hart's version of Natural Law.[3] It is for this reason that Hart's

[1] This is a fairly close paraphrase of Hart, ibid., pp. 89–95. Hart's debt here to Locke's discussion of the 'inconveniences' of the state of nature which are remedied by the institution of government performing legislative, executive and judicial functions should be obvious.

[2] ibid., p. 193. cf. Hume on the 'artificial', but 'not arbitrary' character of the laws of nature in the TREATISE, Bk. III, Part II, Section I.

[3] Kelsen discusses just such a system—a theologically based moral code—in terms of his notion of a basic norm in *On the Basic Norm* 47 CALIFORNIA LAW REVIEW 107 (1959).

claim to have isolated four features of morality which distinguish it from law (as well as other forms of social organization) is important in the present context. For it is only if such features exist that Hart may claim to have provided a concept of *law* which is not also a concept of (at least certain kinds of) morality. The four distinguishing features to which Hart calls attention are the following: (a) Moral rules are essentially thought to be important. A legal rule which nobody believed it important to retain would remain a valid law until it was repealed. 'It would, on the other hand', states Hart, 'be absurd to think of a rule as part of the morality of a society even though no one thought it any longer important or worth maintaining'.[1] (b) Moral rules are essentially immune from deliberate change; there are no analogues in morality to the legal processes of enactment and repeal. (c) Offences against moral rules have a voluntary character in the sense that 'legal reponsibility is not necessarily excluded by the demonstration that an accused person could not have kept the law which he has broken; by contrast, in morals "I could not help it" is always an excuse, although not of course a justification'.[2] (d) '(M)oral pressure is characteristically, though not exclusively, exerted not by threats or by appeals to fear or interest, but by reminders of the moral character of the action contemplated and of the demands of morality.'[3]

The broad outlines of Hart's concept of law are, I believe, faithfully represented by (1), (2), and (3) above, rather than by (1) alone, and it is for this reason that one cannot attribute to Hart a definition of 'legal system' solely in terms of a union of primary and secondary rules.

What might be suggested, though, is that Hart is implicitly committed to the view not that (1) alone, but (1), (2), and (3) taken together, may be restated in terms of a set of necessary and sufficient conditions for the existence of a legal system. Although this latter construal of Hart's analysis is *prima facie* quite plausible, I shall argue in the next section that it would ignore one of his most important insights into the nature of law, for Hart has quite clearly perceived that the concept of a legal system is not to be elucidated by a real definition.

[1] HART, THE CONCEPT OF LAW 171.
[2] ibid., p. 174.
[3] ibid., p. 175.

V

Although I suspect that they are far fewer in number than many philosophers seem to suppose, there are words which are susceptible of real definition. That is to say, one can associate with them a set of necessary and sufficient conditions for their correct application, and this simply upon the basis of a more or less direct examination of their use in the language.[1] There are other terms, though, such that few, if any, of the conditions associated with them (i.e., satisfied in the standard or paradigm cases of their correct application) are individually necessary, and those which are necessary are not jointly sufficient. They represent, in short, what Professor Putnam has aptly labeled 'cluster concepts':

Suppose one makes a list of the attributes $P_1$, $P_2$ . . . that go to make up a normal man. One can raise successively the questions 'Could, there be a man without $P_1$?' 'Could there be a man without $P_2$?' and so on. The answer in each case might be 'Yes', and yet it seems absurd that the word 'man' has no meaning at all . . . the meaning in such a case is given by a cluster of properties. To abandon a large number of these properties, or what is tantamount to the same thing, to radically change the extension of the term 'man', would be felt as an arbitrary change in its meaning. On the other hand, if most of the properties in the cluster are present in any single case, then under suitable circumstances we should be inclined to say that what we had to deal with was a man.[2]

Is the term 'legal system' similar in this respect to what Putnam claims about the term 'man'; does it, in other words, represent a cluster concept? In his 'Theory and Definition in Jurisprudence', Hart quite clearly gives an affirmative answer to this question:

. . . I am not sure that in the case of concepts so complex as that of a legal system we can pick out any characteristics, save the most obvious and uninteresting ones, and say they are necessary. Much of the tiresome logomachy over whether or not international law or primitive law is really law has sprung from the effort to find a considerable set of necessary criteria for the application of the expression 'legal system'. Whereas I think that all that can be found are a set of criteria of which a few are obviously necessary (e.g., there must be rules) but

---

[1] But *only* 'more or less' direct; one must, 'indirectly', be able to discount mistakes, slips of the tongue, etc.

[2] Hilary Putnam, *The Analytic and the Synthetic* 3 MINNESOTA STUDIES IN THE PHILOSOPHY OF SCIENCE 378 (Herbert Feigl and Grover Maxwell, eds., Minneapolis: University of Minnesota Press, 1962).

the rest form a sub-set of criteria of which everything called a legal system satisfies some but only standard or normal cases satisfy all.[1]

After listing a number of such criteria, Hart concludes that 'in the case of a concept so complex . . . we can do no more than identify the conditions present in the standard or paradigm case and consider under what circumstances the removal of any one of these conditions would render the whole pointless or absurd'.[2] Rather than having abandoned this earlier view in *The Concept of Law*, it is precisely this program which Hart may there be viewed as having carried out. For consider the following:

(1) Although the existence of a rule of recognition is said to constitute the 'foundations' of a legal system, Hart does not claim that its existence is *necessary* for the existence of a legal system. Any well-developed system of municipal law will be found to have one, but 'it is possible to imagine a society without a legislature, courts, or officials of any kind', one which would 'live by . . . primary rules alone'.[3] What Hart does here is simply to carry out his program of (a) noting under what circumstances such a society 'could live successfully by such a regime of unofficial rules',[4] and (b) considering in what ways under any other circumstances 'such a simple form of social control must prove defective and will require supplementation'.[5] Hart thus writes that

The proof that 'binding' rules in any society exist, is simply that they are thought of, spoken of, and function as such.[6]

It is, therefore, a mistake to suppose that a basic rule or rule of recognition is a generally necessary condition of the existence of rules of obligation or 'binding' rules. This is not a necessity, but a luxury, found in advanced social systems whose members not merely come to accept separate rules piecemeal, but are committed to the acceptance in

---

[1] *Proceedings of the Aristotelian Society* 251–2 (Supp. Vol. 29, 1955).

[2] ibid., p. 253. To those familiar with Wittgenstein's notion of 'family resemblances' I would like to point out the following: The notion of a cluster concept is quite different, as may be seen by the fact that it is possible to describe a standard or paradigm case of a legal system, but not, according to Wittgenstein, a standard or paradigm case of a game which can serve as a paradigm for any other typical case. E.g., a paradigm case of a card game, such as bridge, can not serve as a paradigm for the quite different kind of game of which baseball is an instance.

[3] HART, THE CONCEPT OF LAW 89.      [4] ibid., p. 90.      [5] ibid.

[6] ibid., p. 226.

advance of general classes of rule, marked out by general criteria of validity.[1]

(2) That any viable legal system must provide some minimal protection for persons, property, and promises through a system of mutual forbearances enforced by sanctions is *not* taken by Hart to constitute a necessary definitional criterion for the existence of a legal system. Hart in fact emphasizes that the realization that this is only what he calls a 'natural necessity' provides a way of avoiding 'certain misleading dichotomies which often obscure the discussion of the characteristics of law'.[2] In a passage which I believe is of some considerable general significance Hart continues:

We shall no longer have to choose between two unsuitable alternatives which are often taken as exhaustive: on the one hand that of saying that this is required by 'the' meaning of the words 'law' or 'legal system', and on the other that of saying that it is 'just a fact' that most legal systems do provide for sanctions. Neither of these alternatives is satisfactory.... For it is a truth of some importance that for the adequate description not only of law but of many other social institutions, a place must be reserved, besides definitions and ordinary statements of fact, for a third category of statements: those the truth of which is contingent on human beings and the world they live in retaining the salient characteristics which they have.[3]

One thing to which Hart has definitely not committed himself, then, either explicitly or implicitly, is a real definition of 'legal system'. And this for the reason that he clearly realizes that the concept of a legal system is what Professor Putnam has called a 'cluster concept'. In other words, few among the large cluster of conditions associated with the existence of a standard or normal case of a well-developed system of municipal law are individually necessary, and these are not jointly sufficient, for the correct application of the expression 'legal system'.[4]

## VI

'What is law?', we have seen, can represent a request for a descrip-

[1] ibid., p. 229. That Hart would be willing to describe at least some cases of sets of primary rules existing alone as *legal systems* is, I believe, made clear by his discussion of international law in Ch. X.    [2] ibid., p. 194.    [3] ibid., p. 195.

[4] That the expression 'legal system' is not amenable to a *real definition* naturally does not mean that a particular *explication* or *rational reconstruction* of it might not prove to be useful within a given well-defined context of inquiry. cf. JULIUS STONE, LEGAL SYSTEM AND LAWYERS' REASONINGS 168 (1964).

tion of the nature, the essence, the most important feature or features of a legal system. There is no room for doubt as to whether or not Hart is committed to an answer to this form of the question in terms of the union of primary and secondary rules. Not only does Hart state that 'their union may be justly regarded as the "essence" of law', but the power of illumination which he attributes to this notion of the union of primary and secondary rules seems to know no limits. Although Hart adds a weak caveat to the effect that their combination 'cannot *by itself* illuminate every problem',[1] he does boast that:

Not only are the specifically legal concepts with which the lawyer is professionally concerned, such as those of obligation and rights, validity and source of law, legislation and jurisdiction, and sanction, best elucidated in terms of this combination of elements. The concepts (which bestride both law and political theory) of the state, of authority, and of an official require a similar analysis if the obscurity which still lingers around them is to be dissipated.[2]

In Section III, it was noted that Hart's distinction between primary and secondary rules is actually highly ambiguous, and it was further claimed that the form in which the distinction is used by Hart will depend upon the problem which Hart is discussing. If this claim is correct—and I believe that any reader of Hart's book can easily verify its correctness by reviewing the index of that book—Hart's contention that he has found in the union of primary and secondary rules 'the key to the science of jurisprudence' which eluded Austin must be rejected. The great explanatory power which this combination of elements appears to Hart to have is simply an illusion which rests upon the multiple ambiguity of the distinction between primary and secondary rules. Indeed, not only is it the case that there is no *one form* of the distinction between primary and secondary rules, and thus no such thing as *the* essence or nature of law; there are also problems in which even Hart is keenly interested in the formulation and solution of which *no form* of the distinction seems to be of the slightest relevance. In respect to this latter point, from which it of course also follows that the notion of the union of primary and secondary rules does not provide 'the key to the science of jurisprudence', let us consider

[1] HART, THE CONCEPT OF LAW 97.
[2] ibid., p. 95.

Hart's valuable discussion of the notion of obligation in *The Concept of Law*.

Austin, we know, attempted to elucidate the concept of a legal rule in terms of the notions of a command and habitual obedience. The American Legal Realists, on the other hand, questioned the very existence of authoritative rules of law and were led to the predictive analysis of validity epitomized by Holmes' dictum that 'The prophecies of what the courts will do in fact, and nothing more pretentious, are . . . the law'.[1] A recurrent theme running throughout Professor Hart's work is an important and well-developed argument to the effect that both of these misconceptions of law are based upon a systematic neglect of what Hart calls the 'internal aspect' of legal rules. Neither Austin nor the Realists, Hart points out, are able to reconstruct the all important notion of *observing a rule* or the closely related concept of *having an obligation to obey a rule*. Where a legal rule exists, Hart argues, it will typically be regarded by the majority of those subject to it with certain 'reflective critical attitudes' which distinguish its *internal* aspect from the mere *external* fact of its observance. These attitudes are displayed by mutual *demands* for conformity to the rule when deviation has occurred or seems likely to do so, in *criticisms* of actual deviations, and in the *acceptance* of such deviation as justifiable grounds for this criticism. It is extremely important to note, firstly, that these are purely behavioral criteria, and, secondly, that the legal obligation which they evidence has no necessary connection with moral obligation.

The fact that Hart does not associate the obligatory aspect of legal rules with any *feelings* of obligation which anyone may have concerning them, as do writers such as A. L. Goodhart and Alf Ross,[2] is repeatedly emphasized:

The internal aspect of rules is often misrepresented as a mere matter of 'feelings' in contrast to externally observable behavior . . . such feelings are neither necessary nor sufficient for the existence of 'binding' rules.[3]

[1] Oliver Wendell Holmes, *The Path of the Law* 10 HARVARD LAW REVIEW 461 (1897).

[2] See A. L. Goodhart, *An Apology for Jurisprudence* INTERPRETATIONS OF MODERN LEGAL PHILOSOPHIES 290 (Paul Sayre, ed., 1957); and Alf Ross, op. cit., Ch. 2.

[3] HART, THE CONCEPT OF LAW 56.

As to whether or not there is any necessary connection between legal and moral obligation, Hart has stated that

it is an aberration of juristic theory to insist that what is at the root of every legal system is a general recognition of a *moral* obligation to obey the law so that there is a necessary or analytic connection and not merely an empirical one between the statement that a legal system exists and the statement that most of the population recognizes a moral obligation to obey the law.[1]

It appears to me to be Hart's position that the most that can be claimed is that the officials of the system manifest the reflective critical attitudes mentioned above to the rules of recognition, change, and adjudication, and that there be general obedience to those primary rules which are valid according to the criteria contained in the rule of recognition. And what must be noted is that

. . . . both this general obedience and the further use of and attitudes to the law may be motivated by fear, inertia, admiration of tradition, or long sighted calculation of selfish interests as well as by recognition of moral obligation. As long as the general complex practice is there, this is enough to answer affirmatively the inquiry whether a legal system exists. The question of what motivates the practice, though important, is an independent inquiry.[2]

It might be claimed, in the light of Hart's minimal version of natural law in *The Concept of Law*, that he has departed from the earlier views expressed above, and that he is now committed to holding that (a) any *viable* legal system must satisfy certain minimal moral requirements, and that (b) there is therefore a moral obligation to support any *viable* legal system. And this, it might be said, implies that there is at least one good reason to obey any valid rule of obligation arising within a viable legal system, although this moral obligation might be overridden by conflicting obligations. I do not believe that this is an acceptable interpretation of Hart's position. Satisfaction of Hart's minimal requirements of natural law is quite consistent with the existence of such oppression and iniquity that the legal system as a whole could not be said to be worthy of support. All that Hart claims is that 'a society to be viable must offer some of its members a system of mutual

---

[1] *Legal and Moral Obligation*, ESSAYS IN MORAL PHILOSOPHY 89 (A. I. Melden, ed., 1958).       [2] ibid., pp. 92–3.

forbearances', which, he notes, means that those benefiting from these forbearances may voluntarily cooperate in the creation of means of coercion which

may be used to subdue and maintain, in a position of permanent inferiority, a subject group whose size, relatively to the master group, may be large or small, depending on the means of coercion, solidarity, and discipline available to the latter, and the helplessness or inability to organize of the former. For those thus oppressed there may be nothing in the system to command their loyalty but only things to fear. They are its victims, not its beneficiaries.[1]

Now the point which I wish to make here is simply this: If it is understood in the manner sketched above, this valuable distinction between the internal and external aspect of legal rules, and all of the important points which Hart makes on the basis of it, is—and must be—quite independent of any form of the distinction between primary and secondary rules in general, and of the existence of a rule of recognition in particular. We have seen (in Section V) that Hart does not claim that the existence of a rule of recognition is necessary for the existence of binding rules of obligation, but rather that he believes it is 'a luxury, found in advanced social systems'. Hart even takes great pains to caution against the attribution of this luxury to societies which in fact do not enjoy it:

There is indeed something comic in the efforts made to fashion a basic rule for the most simple forms of social structure which exist without one. It is as if we were to insist that a naked savage *must* really be dressed in some invisible variety of modern dress. Unfortunately, there is also here a standing possibility of confusion. We may be persuaded to treat as a basic rule, something which is an empty repetition of the mere fact that the society concerned (whether of individuals or states) observes certain standards of conduct as obligatory rules.[2]

There is surely no room for doubt, then, that Hart would agree with my contention that the distinction between the internal and external aspects of legal rules is in fact independent of any distinction between primary and secondary rules. But why *must* this be the case? If the internal aspect of primary rules could only be explained on the basis of the existence of secondary rules, there would have to be tertiary rules to explain the binding aspect of secondary

---

[1] HART, THE CONCEPT OF LAW 196–7.                    [2] ibid., p. 230.

rules, and further rules to explain the internal aspect of tertiary rules, and so on *ad infinitum. For it is the secondary rules themselves which are the preeminent examples of rules which have this internal aspect.* Hart admits, in fact, that it is *only* the secondary rules which must be regarded with the reflective critical attitudes which he describes, and they need be regarded in this way only by the officials of the system in question. As far as 'the man in the street' is concerned, he need only obey (for the most part) the primary rules which are valid according to the system's criteria of validity; indeed, it is only realistic to assume that he will normally have only the faintest idea of the nature of the complex set of secondary rules upon which the whole system is based. (Cf. the first quotation from Hart in Section IV above.[1])

Concerning Professor Hart's claim to have found in the union of primary and secondary rules the most important feature of a legal system—'the key to the science of jurisprudence' which eluded Austin—I believe that we may fairly conclude the following: (1) The distinction between primary and secondary rules, especially in the form in which we have primarily discussed it, is an important distinction with considerable explanatory power in regard to a number of traditional problems in legal philosophy; but (2) There is ample evidence that quite different forms of the distinction will prove to be equally valuable in dealing with other problems; and (3) There are many important problems—even ones in which Hart himself is very much interested, which will not be illuminated by any form of the distinction. Hart has given us *a* valuable key to the science of jurisprudence, then, but that is all. He could not have given us *the* key, for *the* key to the science of jurisprudence does not exist; like the ubiquity of Austin's sovereign, it is a myth.

## VII

Austin's effort to 'determine the province of jurisprudence' was, as Austin himself explicitly notes,[2] an attempt to provide a definition of '(valid) positive law'. And in opposing to the *command* of an

---

[1] This is not to deny Hart's claim, ibid., p. 99, that the recognition of the validity of a primary rule is an internal statement presupposing and manifesting the existence of a secondary rule of recognition.

[2] Austin, op. cit., p. 354.

Austinian sovereign the notion of a *rule* of recognition, Professor Hart is of course providing an explicit answer to the question 'What is law?' as it is understood as an attempt to elicit a definition of the expression 'valid law'. 'To say that a given rule is valid', states Hart, 'is to recognize it as passing all the tests provided by the rule of recognition and so as a rule of the system'.[1] The rule of recognition, Hart argues, is *ultimate*, in the sense that although the validity of other rules is determined by their conformity to the criteria specified in the rule of recognition, there can be no question concerning the validity of the rule of recognition itself. 'Its existence is a matter of fact',[2] not a question of conformity with any higher order rule, and according to Hart it therefore 'can neither be valid nor invalid but is simply accepted as appropriate for use'.[3] The rule of recognition, Hart also notes, is typically composed of a number of criteria and it is usually (although not necessarily) the case that one of these criteria is *supreme*. That is,

. . . rules identified by reference to it are still recognized as rules of the system, even if they conflict with rules identified by reference to the other criteria, whereas rules identified by reference to the latter are not so recognized if they conflict with the rules identified by reference to the supreme criterion.[4]

I believe that there is little doubt that the notion of an ultimate rule of recognition specifying the authoritative sources of law within a given legal system has considerable explanatory power, and it is clear that a proper understanding of its nature permits Hart to resolve many of the difficulties which beset the theories of his predecessors. In spite of this, though, I do not believe that Hart has provided a satisfactory analysis of the concept of a valid law, for it is not difficult to see that conformity with all of the criteria of which the rule of recognition consists is neither a necessary nor a sufficient condition for the validity of a legal rule:

(1) We have seen (in Section V above) that Hart does *not* claim that the existence of a rule of recognition is a necessary condition for the existence of a legal system. But one condition which he *does* admit is 'obviously necessary' for the existence of a legal system is that there be *rules*. Legal rules. i.e., *valid laws*. Since the existence of a rule of recognition is not a necessary condition

---

[1] HART, THE CONCEPT OF LAW 100.    [2] ibid., p. 107.
[3] ibid., p. 105, and generally pp. 102–7.    [4] ibid., p. 103.

for the existence of a legal system, then, it cannot be a necessary condition for the existence of a valid law.

(2) More importantly, consider a well-developed system of municipal law which does enjoy the 'luxury' of a rule of recognition. Although on the basis of Hart's analysis one can then of course ask meaningful questions about the validity of subordinate rules within the system, Hart claims that it is not meaningful to question the validity of the rule of recognition itself. We can of course ask whether or not a particular rule formulation correctly represents the rule of recognition which is in fact in use within the system; we can ask whether or not it is a good rule, or if a better one might be devised; but what we cannot do is speak of its validity.

We only need the word 'validity', and commonly only use it, to answer questions which arise *within* a system of rules where the status of a rule as a member of the system depends on its satisfying certain criteria provided by the rule of recognition. No such question can arise as to the validity of the very rule of recognition which provides the criteria; it can neither be valid nor invalid but is simply accepted as appropriate for use in this way.[1]

'(T)he rule of recognition', Hart concludes, 'exists *only* as a complex, but normally concordant, practice of the courts, officials, and private persons in identifying the law by reference to certain criteria. Its existence is a matter of fact'.[2]

What Hart has done here is to make the rule of recognition *sovereign* in a way which is strictly analogous to the sovereignty of the determinate person or persons constituting the Austinian sovereign. For Austin, the only important *relation* is that of *habitual obedience*; for Hart, the only important *relation* is that of *rule accordance*. Just as the Austinian sovereign does not stand in the relation of habitual obedience to any other person or persons, so Hart's sovereign rule[3] of recognition does not stand in the relation of rule accordance to any other legal rule. And just as we could not meaningfully question the legal validity of the commands of an Austinian sovereign, neither can we question the legal validity of Hart's rule of recognition. Rules of recognition,

---

[1] ibid., pp. 105–6.    [2] ibid., p. 107 (italics mine).
[3] Von Wright captures Hart's notion of validity exactly and refers to 'a norm which cannot be traced back to any other norm' as a 'sovereign norm'. See GEORG HENRICK VON WRIGHT, NORM AND ACTION 199 (1963).

like Austinian sovereigns, just exist; while the latter die, the former only fade away (into disuse).

Now the difficulty here is simply this. Hart takes considerable pains to insist that the rule of recognition, unlike Kelsen's 'basic norm', is not an *extra-legal* juristic hypothesis, but rather *a rule of positive law*. And of course the various constitutional rules which together comprise the rule of recognition *are* rules of positive law—*valid* rules of positive law in the very sense of 'valid' which Hart is attempting to explicate. Hart's definition of 'valid law', then, must be incorrect, for he is not *stipulating* the meaning of a new technical term, but attempting to reflect in a real definition long standing usage according to which constitutional law is really valid law. Even where a rule of recognition exists, then, conformity with it cannot be a *necessary* condition for the existence of a valid law.

(3) Conformity with the rule of recognition is not a sufficient condition for the validity of a legal rule either, for at least some of the other conditions which are normally associated with the existence of a valid legal rule must be satisfied as well. Consider, for instance, a statute which is passed by a competent legislature in conformity with all of the procedural and substantive requirements of the constitution, but which is (a) not promulgated, (b) not obeyed, (c) not enforced by police or prosecutors, and (d) never applied in the courts. If one were asked to describe 'the law' on the subject to which this statute pertained, I submit, one would not be likely to include it.

Hart might reply that although such a statute is not *in fact* being obeyed, enforced, or applied by the courts, the fact that it is in accord with the rule of recognition distinguishes it from other rules which are not in that it *ought* to be applied by the courts. The concept of a valid law, in other words, might be said to be the concept of a rule which the courts ought to apply. And if the notion of validity were to be understood in this way, conformity with the rule of recognition would of course constitute a *sufficient* condition for the existence of a valid law. But it would still fail to be a necessary condition. Not only do objections (1) and (2) above show this, but so does an additional objection which now comes to light.

(4) Hart admits—as he must—that in the so-called 'hard cases' a uniquely correct judicial decision will *not* be determined by an appeal to the authoritative sources of law specified by the rule of

recognition. Such cases may involve a conflict among, or the need for the interpretation of, rules which are formally valid in Hart's sense, or it may simply be that there is a 'gap' in the law in the sense that there is no formally valid rule which is directly applicable to the facts of the case. But in such cases, Hart notes, judges must nevertheless 'deploy some acceptable general principle as a reasoned basis for decision',[1] and he even suggests that what he calls *permissive sources* of law provide the criteria which make it possible to distinguish between those principles which are 'acceptable' and those which are not. It is to these permissive sources which the judge must appeal, states Hart, when

no statute or other formal source of law determines the case before him ... The legal system does not require him to use these sources, but it is accepted as perfectly proper that he should do so. They are therefore more than merely historical or causal influences since ... recognized as 'good reasons' for decisions.[2]

Now it seems clear that in at least some—if not all—of these hard cases one may meaningfully speak of a rule which is determined by these permissive sources of law as being *the* rule which the court *ought* to apply. But if this is the case, and if a valid law is said to be a law which the courts ought to apply, conformity to the rule of recognition therefore cannot be a necessary condition for the existence of a valid law.

I believe it is fair to conclude, then, that Hart has not provided a satisfactory definition of the expression 'valid law', for conformity to the rule of recognition is not a necessary and sufficient condition for the existence (validity) of a legal rule.

## VIII

The reason why Hart and many others have failed to provide a satisfactory definition of 'valid law' is, I believe, that the concept of a valid law, like that of a legal system, is a cluster concept. Associated with the standard or normal case of a valid law, in other words, is a large cluster of conditions such that few, if any, of them are individually necessary, and these are not jointly sufficient, for the existence of a valid law. If one is concerned to elucidate the concept

---

[1] HART, THE CONCEPT OF LAW 200.    [2] ibid., pp. 246–7.

of legal validity, then, one must attempt to identify the relevant conditions associated with standard cases of valid laws, and to describe the difference it would make (in terms of the factors in which one is interested) if any one of these conditions were to be absent in a rule which was (as far as possible) just like a normal case of a valid law in all other respects. This is precisely the sort of program which I suggested Hart has carried out with respect to the concept of a legal system in *The Concept of Law*; it is unfortunate that he did not appreciate the fact that such a program, rather than an attempt at real definition, was equally well suited to the concept of legal validity.

If one is interested in the likelihood that a given legal prohibition will be generally obeyed, for instance, one should inquire whether sanctions are attached to its violation, whether it meets with general moral approval, whether it is likely that it will be strictly enforced, etc. It is in the answers to specific questions such as these that one must be interested in the context of any serious inquiry, and once these answers are given, there is no need to go on and ask the further question 'Is it a valid law?' Once one has been told which of the conditions associated with the standard cases of valid laws are present in a particular case, and which are not, one knows all that there is to know.

What is needed, I submit, is a broader terminology; the single term 'valid law' is simply insufficient to cover the distinctions which need to be made within the context of any particular problem, and there are no grounds for the claim that any one of these distinctions is *the* distinction. When a lawyer is advising a client as to how he may conduct his affairs so as to remain out of court, for example, his chief concern must clearly be with the rules which he believes will be *enforced* by police and prosecutors, or (in other contexts) with those rules which the people with whom his client is dealing believe the courts will apply in civil suits. But if the lawyer is advising his client as to his chances of winning a law suit, he will then be making a *prediction* about what rules the courts will *in fact apply*. And if the lawyer ends up defending his client in court, he will then be concerned with convincing the judge that there are certain rules which he is *bound*, or which he simply *ought*, to apply. But if the lawyer assumes the scholarly role of constitutional lawyer, and perhaps writes an article for a law journal, he may then urge that one of the rules which the lower courts are in fact applying, and which they are bound to apply, should be declared unconstitutional by the Supreme Court. Suppose it is a statute which he believes is unconstitutional. His reasons may be of various sorts, and he will be sure to make them explicit: He may believe that the body which enacted the statute was not *competent* to do so; or that, although competent, it did not follow the correct *procedures*; or that, although the correct procedures were followed by a competent body, the enacted statute is in violation of a *substantive right* which is constitutionally guaranteed.

Such distinctions as these exist, they are important, and the terminology in which to express them has been available for some time. There are no reasons to supplant this terminology, and thus blur the distinctions which can be made in terms of it, by an oversimplified dichotomy between 'valid' and 'invalid' laws. There is no such thing as *the essence* of a valid law, and where a particular rule lacks some of the features associated with the standard cases of legal rules, while it shares others, the thing to do is to *describe* the similarities and differences, and not to either under or over-emphasize them, while at the same time concealing what they actually are, by stamping what is an admittedly atypical case with a useless label. The description and criticism of what courts do, in short, is not as simple a thing as the endorsement of a toaster with the Good Housekeeping Seal of Approval.

## XI

The final form of the question 'What is law?' which we have distinguished, 'What is a good reason for a judicial decision?', is one to which Hart's claims concerning the nature and status of the rule of recognition are directly relevant in a number of ways. And although I believe that there is much that is both important and correct in what Hart either explicitly states or directly implies concerning the nature of the justification of the judicial decision, I shall also suggest that there are a number of respects in which it is unacceptable.

A legal rule which is in conformity with all of the criteria contained in the rule of recognition, and thus formally valid in Hart's sense, is one which judges not only *ought* to apply, but one which they are *bound* to apply. And in the vast majority of cases, Hart quite clearly perceives, the correct judicial decision is simply that decision which follows from the application of a formally valid legal rule to the legal facts of the case.

But we have seen above that Hart realizes that the typical 'easy' case is not the only kind of case calling for judicial decision, and that there are a number of different sorts of 'hard' cases in which a uniquely correct decision will not be dictated by an appeal to formally valid legal rules. Here, Hart suggests, judges must appeal to what he calls 'permissive sources of law' in order to justify their decisions, and although Hart says little more on the matter, there is a clear suggestion that what the judge will often have to turn to in such cases are extra-legal moral standards accepted in the community.

Judicial decision often involves a choice between moral values, and not merely the application of some single outstanding moral principle; for it is folly to believe that where the meaning of the law is in doubt, morality always has a clear answer to offer. At this point judges may . . . make a choice which is neither arbitrary nor mechanical; and here often display characteristic judicial virtues, the special appropriateness of which to legal decision explains why some feel reluctant to call such judicial activity 'legislative'.[1]

What Hart says here, although sketchy, is unambiguous, and while it might be unfair to take him to task concerning an issue to which he pays but little attention and on which he offers few *arguments*, it nevertheless seems to me that two observations should be made. (1) There are those who have argued that even if judges must at some point appeal to extra-legal standards in order to justify their decisions, it is far from 'folly' to believe that one may meaningfully speak of a uniquely correct decision. Indeed, it seems to me that the issue here is one of the most interesting and difficult ones connected with the general problem of the justification of the judicial decision, and I am sure that no answer as short as Hart's will withstand serious scrutiny.[2] (2) The claim that judges are sometimes justified in appealing to extra-legal standards which are in no way already established as part of the law, although often heard, is seldom closely examined. Once this view is subjected to a close examination, I believe that equally

[1] ibid., p. 200.

[2] See, for instance: Ronald Dworkin and Gerald MacCallum, *Symposium on Judicial Discretion* 60 JOURNAL OF PHILOSOPHY 638 (1963), and my own *The Justification of the Judicial Decision*, 78 ETHICS 171 (1968).

plausible alternative views come to light. There are those, for instance, who would argue that no judicial decision is legally justified unless it can be subsumed under a rule which is itself in some way implied or established by existing legal principles and policies.[1]

The chief difficulties which I find in what Hart states or implies concerning the nature of the justification of the judicial decision stem directly from what he says about the status of the rule of recognition. Here, more than at any other place in *The Concept of Law*, it appears to me as if Hart's usually careful and penetrating analysis has given way to claims which are hasty, oversimplified, and often obviously incorrect.

The multiple criteria of which the rule of recognition consists are of course *legal* (constitutional) rules; and it is not infrequently that these criteria will be the subject of *legal* controversies which come before the highest courts. In the famous case of *Marbury* v. *Madison*,[2] for instance, the issue of law before the United States Supreme Court was whether or not that Court had the legal right to review the content of statutes passed by Congress as well as to examine whether or not they were enacted according to the forms prescribed in the Constitution. In the equally famous British case of *London Street Tramways* v. *L. C. C.*[3] the House of Lords affirmed that it is bound by its own past decisions, and this rule is almost as important a part of the ultimate rule of recognition in the British system as is the existence of judicial review in our own. Now Professor Hart is of course aware of the existence of such cases; of the fact that '... the ultimate rule of a legal system may ... be in doubt ... and courts may resolve the doubt',[4] but it seems to me that on his view, which is that the existence of the rule of recognition is 'only a matter of fact', there is no room left for a satisfactory account of what qualify as good reasons for resolving such doubts in some ways rather than others. It is not that questions about the rule of recognition can *not* be, from the standpoint of someone outside the system, questions of fact; it is that such questions *can* also be asked from within the system, and that when they are, they are questions of law which call for judicial

---

[1] See Israel Scheffler, *On Justification and Commitment* 51 JOURNAL OF PHILOSOPHY 180 (1954), and Sartorius, op. cit.

[2] 1 Cranch. 137, 2 L. ED. 60 (1803).

[3] 1898 A.C. 375.  [4] HART, THE CONCEPT OF LAW 145.

decisions which it must at least in some cases be correct to describe
as either justified or unjustified. Although considerations of
judicial practice will naturally be relevant, the point is that there
will be *other* good reasons for the judicial decision in cases of
constitutional law, and it is the existence of these considerations
which Hart's view that 'the rule of recognition exists only as a
complex . . . practice' seems to deny. Although Hart recognizes a
distinction between permissive and authoritative sources of law
in the hard cases which involve the interpretation of statutes or
precedents, he implies that the constitutional cases are *so hard*
that no such distinction is relevant. As Hart himself admits, he has
accepted both the rule scepticism and the essentially predictive
analysis of the realists as a correct account of these *very hard*
cases:

The truth may be that, when courts settle previously unenvisaged
questions concerning the most fundamental constitutional rules, they
*get* their authority to decide them accepted after the questions have
arisen and the decisions have been given. Here all that succeeds is
success.[1]

Hart is of course correct that to one who has adopted the
*external* point of view, as he calls it, the existence of a constitution
will for the most part consist in the largely concordant *practice* of
courts, other officials, and private citizens in the identification of
particular rules and decisions as being ones which place them under
legal obligations. What Hart fails to appreciate the significance of,
though, are the *results* of the fact that the practice which is being
referred to here is one in which the constitutional rules are being
used *within the system* as *critical standards* of both official and
private behavior. For once people begin to use a set of regularities
as standards of their own behavior, I submit, a question can arise as
to whether or not any particular member of this set is the *correct*
standard to use in a particular situation. And this question reduces
neither to the question 'Is this a standard which is in fact being
used?' nor to the question 'Is this a good standard to have, or
would it be a better institution if a different one were to take its
place?'. One can ask of *any* legal rule 'Is this the rule which the
judge, *qua* judge, ought to apply?', and constitutional rules are no
exception. As Morris Cohen once put it, '*Any* decision may be

criticized on the ground that it is not consistent with the principles generally recognized or embodied in specific statutes or repeated previous decisions. . .'.[1]

None of this is meant to imply that the correctness of the *whole
system* of rules can be called into question at once; nor does it mean
that each judge is in the position to revise each rule in any way.
And although I would urge that the question of whether or not a
given rule is the right rule is very different from the question of
whether or not it is in fact being followed, I do not mean to imply
that what is evidence for its existence can not also serve as one
sort of *good reason* for claiming that it is correct. The point which
I wish to stress is simply that even if a given rule is in fact being
followed by the courts, other officials, and private citizens, this
alone is by no means *conclusive* of its correctness. In the case of
constitutional rules, of equal importance will be the way in which
a particular criterion of validity accords with *the total judicial
theory of the constitution*, with the background of historical documents, judicial practice, and judicial interpretation of these
documents and this practice. Alf Ross, who claims that in both
law and empirical science '(t)he question is whether the particular
law is compatible with the hitherto accepted system . . . (and)
nothing is established beyond doubt',[2] suggests just this point.

This view, that the existence of constitutional law depends at
least in part on the practice of *courts* and *officials*, might appear to
involve a vicious circularity. For courts and officials, it might be
argued, are themselves *created by* constitutional law. According to
Professor Rawls, for instance, legal and legal-like institutions are
*defined by* constitutive rules the existence of which is *logically prior*
to the existence of the institutions which they define.[3] But an
objection of this sort, I submit, rests upon a subtle confusion: it is
not the constitutional rules, but the constitutional practice, which
is logically prior to the authority of the state, and the two are of
course by no means equivalent. Before this authority is established,
courts and officials exist only as identifiable bodies and individuals
which exercise powers to which, in the beginning, they can claim
no legal right. Their authority is established only after their *de*

---

[1] MORRIS R. COHEN, REASON AND LAW 89 (1961) (italics mine).

[2] ROSS, ON LAW AND JUSTICE, p. 36, n. 3.

[3] John Rawls, *Two Concepts of Rules* 64 PHILOSOPHICAL REVIEW 3 (1955),
especially page 32.

*facto* existence is established, and it is the courts and officials which themselves establish this authority by employing as critical standards the constitutional rules which grant it to them. What are at first nothing more than mere descriptions, from Hart's external point of view, of constitutional practice, therefore *become* rules of constitutional law. It is at this stage, when a whole body of constitutional practice is in the process of becoming constitutional law, that Hart is correct in describing the situation as one in which 'nothing succeeds but success'. But once such a body of constitutional *law* exists, there is, as I have already suggested, a theoretical background which can exercise a considerable degree of systematic control over those judicial decisions which must be made in the very hard cases which hinge upon questions of constitutional law. At this point, Hart's claim that 'the rule of recognition exists only as a complex . . . practice' seems to be patently false; its existence is a question of law, and the answers which courts give to this question in the form of judicial decisions are subject to the same standards of legal correctness as are judicial decisions in other sorts of hard cases.

Most, if not all, of this was accurately perceived by John Salmond:

> . . . the constitution is both a matter of fact and a matter of law . . .
> Constitutional law involves concurrent constitutional practice . . . It is the theory of the constitution, as received by courts of justice . . .
> The constitution as a matter of fact is logically prior to the constitution as a matter of law. In other words, constitutional practice is logically prior to constitutional law . . . No constitution, therefore, can have its source and basis in the law. It has of necessity an extra-legal origin, for there can be no talk of law until some form of constitution has already obtained *de facto* establishment by way of actual usage and operation. When it is once established, but not before, the law can, and will, take notice of it. Constitutional facts will be reflected with more or less accuracy in courts of justice as constitutional law. The law will develop for itself a theory of the constitution, as it develops a theory of most other things which come in question in the administration of justice.[1]

It is unfortunate that Professor Hart, who acknowledges the close resemblance that his conception of a rule of recognition bears to Salmond's notion of an ultimate legal principle,[2] did not play

---

[1] JOHN SALMOND, JURISPRUDENCE 100–1 (edited by Glanville Williams, 11th ed., 1957).    [2] HART, THE CONCEPT OF LAW 245.

closer attention to Salmond's suggestion that judicial notice of constitutional practice will give rise to a *theory* of constitutional law. For it is in terms of such a theory that judicial decisions on hard constitutional questions may be justified; and it is because of the existence of such a theory that one may distinguish—as Hart suggests one can not do—between constitutional practice and constitutional law. Hart's failure here, I believe, stems directly from his preoccupation with the valid-invalid distinction as the primary distinction involved in the justification of the judicial decision. Although Hart has at hand the further distinction between permissive and authoritative sources of law, it is relegated to a footnote and never developed. But it is just this sort of distinction which must be developed and applied if one is to elucidate the justification of the judicial decision in the hard cases, which include, I suggest, the *very* hard cases which involve the criteria of which Hart's rule of recognition consists.[1]

[1] I would like to express my gratitude to Joel Feinberg, Robert Jones, Samuel Shuman, and Gregory Vlastos for their helpful comments on earlier versions of this paper.